DAVID LETTERMAN

★ ★ ★ ★ ★ ★ ★ ★ ★ ★ ★ ★ ★ ★ ★ ★

DAVID LETTERMAN

★ ★ ★ ★ ★ ★ ★ ★ ★ ★ ★ ★ ★ ★ ★ ★ ★ ★ ★

FRANCES LEFKOWITZ

CHELSEA HOUSE PUBLISHERS

New York ★ Philadelphia

CHELSEA HOUSE PUBLISHERS

EDITORIAL DIRECTOR   Richard Rennert
EXECUTIVE MANAGING EDITOR   Karyn Gullen Browne
COPY CHIEF   Robin James
PICTURE EDITOR   Adrian G. Allen
CREATIVE DIRECTOR   Robert Mitchell
ART DIRECTOR   Joan Ferrigno
PRODUCTION MANAGER   Sallye Scott

Pop Culture Legends
SENIOR EDITOR   Kathy Kuhtz Campbell
SERIES DESIGN   Basia Niemczyc

Staff for DAVID LETTERMAN
EDITORIAL ASSISTANT   Scott D. Briggs
PICTURE RESEARCHER   Matthew Dudley
COVER ILLUSTRATION   Daniel O'Leary

First Printing

1 3 5 7 9 8 6 4 2

Library of Congress Cataloging-in-Publication Data

Lefkowitz, Frances.
David Letterman/Frances Lefkowitz.
p. cm.—(Pop culture legends)
Includes bibliographical references and index.
Summary: A biography of the late-night television talk show host, comedian,
and comedy writer who first appeared nationally in 1978 on the Tonight
Show.
ISBN 0-7910-3252-3
        0-7910-3253-1 (pbk.)
1. Letterman, David. 2. Television personalities—United States—Biogra-
phy—Juvenile literature. 3. Comedians—United States—Biography—Ju-
venile literature. [1. Letterman, David. 2. Television personalities. 3.
Comedians.] I. Title II. Series.
PN1992.4.L39L34 1996   95-35142
791.45'028'092—dc20   CIP
[B]   AC

FRONTISPIECE:

On January 14, 1993, David Letterman announces that
he will be leaving the NBC network to host a late-night talk
show on CBS.

Contents ★ ★ ★ ★ ★ ★ ★ ★ ★ ★ ★ ★ ★ ★ ★ ★ ★ ★

A Reflection of Ourselves

Leeza Gibbons

I ENJOY A RARE PERSPECTIVE on the entertainment industry. From my window on popular culture, I can see all that sizzles and excites. I have interviewed legends who have left us, such as Bette Davis and Sammy Davis, Jr., and have brushed shoulders with the names who have caused a commotion with their sheer outrageousness, like Boy George and Madonna. Whether it's by nature or by design, pop icons generate interest, and I think they are a mirror of who we are at any given time.

Who are *your* heroes and heroines, the people you most admire? Outside of your own family and friends, to whom do you look for inspiration and guidance, as examples of the type of person you would like to be as an adult? How do we decide who will be the most popular and influential members of our society?

You may be surprised by your answers. According to recent polls, you will probably respond much differently than your parents or grandparents did to the same questions at the same age. Increasingly, world leaders such as Winston Churchill, John F. Kennedy, Franklin D. Roosevelt, and evangelist Billy Graham have been replaced by entertainers, athletes, and popular artists as the individuals whom young people most respect and admire. In surveys taken during each of the past 15 years, for example, General Norman Schwarzkopf was the only world leader chosen as the number-one hero among high school students. Other names on the elite list joined by General Schwarzkopf included Paula Abdul, Michael Jackson, Michael Jordan, Eddie Murphy, Burt Reynolds, and Sylvester Stallone.

7

More than 30 years have passed since Canadian sociologist Marshall McLuhan first taught us the huge impact that the electronic media has had on how we think, learn, and understand—as well as how we choose our heroes. In the 1960s, Pop artist Andy Warhol predicted that there would soon come a time when every American would be famous for 15 minutes. But if it is easier today to achieve Warhol's 15 minutes of fame, it is also much harder to hold on to it. Reputations are often ruined as quickly as they are made.

And yet, there remain those artists and performers who continue to inspire and instruct us in spite of changes in world events, media technology, or popular tastes. Even in a society as fickle and fast moving as our own, there are still those performers whose work and reputation endure, pop culture legends who inspire an almost religious devotion from their fans.

Why do the works and personalities of some artists continue to fascinate us while others are so quickly forgotten? What, if any, qualities do they share that enable them to have such power over our lives? There are no easy answers to these questions. The artists and entertainers profiled in this series often have little more in common than the enormous influence that each of them has had on our lives.

Some offer us an escape. Artists such as actress Marilyn Monroe, comedian Groucho Marx, and writer Stephen King have used glamour, humor, or fantasy to help us escape from our everyday lives. Others present us with images that are all too recognizable. The uncompromising realism of actor and director Charlie Chaplin and folk singer Bob Dylan challenges us to confront and change the things in our world that most disturb us.

Some offer us friendly, reassuring experiences. The work of animator Walt Disney and late-night talk show host Johnny Carson, for example, provides us with a sense of security and continuity in a changing world. Others shake us up. The best work of composer John Lennon and actor James Dean will always inspire their fans to question and reevaluate the world in which they live.

It is also hard to predict the kind of life that a pop culture legend will lead, or how he or she will react to fame. Popular singers Michael Jackson

and Prince carefully guard their personal lives from public view. Other performers, such as popular singer Madonna, enjoy putting their private lives before the public eye.

What these artists and entertainers do share, however, is the rare ability to capture and hold the public's imagination in a world dominated by mass media and disposable celebrity. In spite of their differences, each of them has somehow managed to achieve legendary status in a popular culture that values novelty and change.

The books in this series examine the lives and careers of these and other pop culture legends, and the society that places such great value on their work. Each book considers the extraordinary talent, the stubborn commitment, and the great personal sacrifice required to create work of enduring quality and influence in today's world.

As you read these books, ask yourself the following questions: How are the careers of these individuals shaped by their society? What role do they play in shaping the world? And what is it that so captivates us about their lives, their work, or the images they present?

Hopefully, by studying the lives and achievements of these pop culture legends, we will learn more about ourselves.

★ 1 ★ Introducing David Letterman

OPERA SINGERS HAVE THE MET, baseball players have Yankee Stadium, country musicians have the Grand Ole Opry, and comedians have the "Tonight Show." For more than three decades this late-night talk show has been a staple of American television and the single most important forum for stand-up comedians. An appearance on the "Tonight Show" is the sign of making it, and aspiring comics pin their hopes on getting a chance to perform alongside the established stars on the roster of this program.

As host of the "Tonight Show," Johnny Carson earned such titles as King of Nighttime TV and King of the Night. Though he retired in 1992, Carson is still one of the most popular and powerful figures in the entertainment world. For 30 years his "Tonight Show" was a model of constancy in a medium known for its rapid changes; no other program in the history of television has lasted as long. Millions of television viewers across the country tuned in nightly to hear sidekick Ed McMahon announce "Heeeere's Johnny!" and watch Carson deliver his acclaimed opening monologue, then sit down at his desk, with the skyline of Hollywood in the background, and

On July 2, 1979, comedian David Letterman performs his opening act during a guest host appearance on Johnny Carson's the "Tonight Show." Letterman performed on the "Tonight Show" for the first time on November 26, 1978, and later said it was the biggest night of his career.

chat with celebrity guests. For some people, watching Carson and his nightly rituals—mugging for the cameras, tapping his pencil, and making jokes about the day's events, his own divorce, or bandleader Doc Severinson's clothes—was as much a part of getting ready for bed as washing their faces and brushing their teeth.

But for aspiring comedians, Johnny Carson was an intimidating figure. He held such power in the entertainment business that he could jump start a comic's career simply by offering five minutes of national exposure on his show. Performing on his program was like taking a test. Passing the test, by impressing Carson, could almost ensure a comedian's success. As David Letterman once said, "Everybody looks to him for his reactions. Comics are sensitive about how he treats them. One I know was upset because Johnny failed to mention his name when

Host Johnny Carson (right) and his sidekick Ed McMahon mug for the cameras during a 1979 broadcast of the "Tonight Show." For many comedians, an appearance on the nightly program is the sign of "making it" in show business.

he finished a routine. 'Do you think that means any-thing?' he asked me."

On November 26, 1978, the familiar red curtains opened and the 31-year-old comedian and comedy writer David Letterman walked onto the stage of the "Tonight Show." To his left was Doc Severinson and the "Tonight Show" band, to his right was Johnny Carson, and in front of him were the studio audience and the video cameras taping his performance for broadcast to millions of view-ers. Letterman, who was always uncomfortable doing stand-up performances, was overcome with nerves. At least he knew his monologue—in the weeks preceding this engagement, the only way to combat his nerves was to practice so much that no matter how he felt the night of the show, he would still be able to deliver his routine. "I knew I had that one cold," he said afterward. "Unless there was an earthquake or a power outage or an assassi-nation, I knew I had that one slick. I did it and it worked beyond my wildest dreams." Fortunately for Letterman, there were no earthquakes in Southern California that night, and he delivered his best four minutes of jokes to an appreciative, applauding audience.

At the end of his routine, Carson, from behind his desk, motioned for Letterman to come over and sit next to him on the guest couch. It was an unexpected honor, as Carson rarely extended such an invitation to the new comics who appeared on his show; usually they got their three to five minutes in the spotlight and then walked offstage. But Carson obviously liked Letterman and wanted to give him another moment of airtime. If being invited to perform on the "Tonight Show" was like getting an A in school, then being asked to chat with Carson onstage was like earning extra credit.

For all of his rehearsing, Letterman had not prepared himself for having a casual conversation with his idol on national television. As he said later, "I sat down and

Johnny Carson is sitting right there, and you're just talking and talking and praying to God that it's over soon, and you're looking around and you're seeing stuff that you've seen on TV for years. And you can't let yourself think for a second or, you know, your head would explode. So you're talking and talking and just praying, 'Oh please go to a commercial, please go to a commercial!' And the next thing you know you're out of there and its just, 'Holy Christ, I was on the 'Tonight' show!'" Finally, Letterman's prayers were answered: it was time for a commercial break and for him to leave the stage.

The biggest night of Letterman's life was over. For Letterman, who had long admired Carson, the night had great personal, as well as professional, significance. As a boy, Letterman had watched Carson on a network television quiz show called "Who Do You Trust?," which Carson hosted from 1958 until 1962 and which sparked Letterman's own interest in pursuing a career in television. According to Letterman, on one episode of the program, "There was one guest who balanced a lawn mower on his chin. . . . And Carson just made fun of him. I thought, 'What a great way to make a living!'" Once Letterman began pursuing his broadcasting career in earnest, his admiration for Carson only grew. "If it had not been for the 'Tonight Show' and Johnny Carson, I wouldn't have a car—probably wouldn't have shoes. But the real reason I look up to the guy is the longer I do this, the more respect I have for him. Show me somebody else in the history of television who has not only survived but also dominated for a quarter of a century. I think if you don't have respect for that, there's something wrong with you."

Letterman, who had worked in radio and television as well as in stand-up comedy, had long fantasized about performing on the "Tonight Show." Comedy writer Merrill Markoe, who lived and worked with Letterman

On March 1, 1956, Johnny Carson, host of the quiz show "Who Do You Trust?", holds up some of the money that came into the studio after he jokingly closed the show by staring into the camera and telling the audience that he was hypnotizing them.
He then told the viewers to "send all your money to Johnny Carson, care of CBS television." As a boy, Letterman watched Carson on television frequently and said it was because of Carson that he chose broadcasting as a career.

for many years, once said, "All the time I knew him, Dave dreamed of going on the 'Tonight' show." His appearance that night in November was literally a dream come true.

How did Letterman feel sitting on the "Tonight Show" couch talking to the King of Late Night? "To suddenly find yourself seated next to him is stunning. You're from Indiana, and you sit there year after year watching Johnny Carson when you're 16, 17 years old, and then the next thing you know, 1978, he's right there." But along with awe and anxiety, the experience also gave Letterman a tremendous jolt of confidence. "It was the most fun I ever had," he said, once it was over.

"There I was holding my own with Johnny Carson. I knew I could hit big league pitching."

In fact, his performance on the "Tonight Show" was more like winning a prize fight. For Letterman, who had taken many risks in trying to establish a career in show business, "It justified, certified, legitimized everything I had done that everybody thought was insane. And nothing that has happened since has come close to that." It was certainly the triumph of his career to date. Before his appearance on the Carson show, the most exposure Letterman had was in minor roles on a handful of short-lived television programs. He spent much of his time writing jokes and then performing them, along with hundreds of other aspiring comedians, at a Los Angeles nightclub called the Comedy Store. This nightclub has become legendary as a breeding ground for fledgling comedians who try out their routines in front of an audience and hope to get noticed by producers and scouts who occasionally come by to check out the talent. It is a place seething with hopes and ambitions, and the atmosphere is often cutthroat. But it was there, at the Comedy Store, that David Letterman's dream of appearing on the "Tonight Show" began to materialize.

"The people at 'The Tonight Show' are very good at dealing with young comedians," Letterman once explained. "They want nothing more than to break another Freddie Prinze [the comedian who went on to star in the television sitcom "Chico and the Man"], and they keep track of everybody." It was at the Comedy Store that producers from the "Tonight Show" first noticed Letterman. "In 1977 the Carson people came to me and said, 'You're not ready.' I said 'Okay, that's fine.' I was just thrilled they'd been watching me. And the last thing you want to do is go on and not be ready. So I kept working and building my act, and the next year, they called for me." In fact, Letterman was glad to have the time to write more material for his act. He had a fear of being unprepared and wanted to make sure he had enough jokes for several engagements, if they came up. By the next year, he had garnered plenty of practice at the Comedy Store, some good exposure on television, and a cache of material. He was ready for the "Tonight Show," and the "Tonight Show" was ready for him.

The one thing he was not ready for was the impact that his brief appearance on the "Tonight Show" would have on every aspect of his life. "I was in a different dimension," he said later. "It's like West Point graduation and your hat's in the air. All those years hanging around the Comedy Store and driving around in your truck and heating up burritos at the 7-Eleven, and drinking warm quarts of beer. All of a sudden it's changed, you're on the 'Tonight' show. It was like a miracle. It turned me upside down. I go to the Comedy Store now and I was an important guy because I had been on the 'Tonight' show. I was one of the chosen few."

That first appearance on the "Tonight Show" was like a stick of dynamite to Letterman's career: it set off a chain of events, each more explosive than the last. First, "King" Carson was so impressed with Letterman that he soon invited him back for a second, then a third, appearance. Then, the "Tonight Show" producers invited him to be a substitute host and fill in for Carson on one of his frequent nights off. Being on the roster of substitute hosts was a highly coveted position among comedians, and Letterman made it to that roster in just a few months, faster than any other guest had. In fact, it was the quickest rise from guest to guest host in the history of the show. As Letterman described it: "During the middle of the third show, producer Fred de Cordova came over and said, 'Have your people call me about hosting.' It was a real numbing experience, having that go through my mind while I was still sitting there, pretending to be part

In May 1992, one week before Carson retired from the "Tonight Show," he invited Letterman back for a guest appearance. Now host of his own late-night talk show, Letterman thanked Carson for his career.

of the show." Soon, he was substituting regularly for Carson, alternating with such established comedians as Joan Rivers and David Brenner.

But Letterman was impressing more than just Carson's people; his frequent appearances on the "Tonight Show" made a lot of influential people take note of him. Before long, he became a hot topic in the press. As he explained, "In California, I was literally living in a one-room apartment on stilts in Laurel Canyon, and I had hosted 'The Tonight Show' a couple times, and then I went away. When I got back to my house in Laurel Canyon, I had mail from people all over the country, and they had all sent clippings carrying the same wire release saying that I would be the next Johnny Carson. I thought, 'Good Lord.' The week before, I was having trouble getting enough money to have the clutch in my truck replaced, and the next week I'm getting clippings saying I'm the next Johnny Carson."

The increased exposure and the stories in the press created a buzz around Letterman that was not wasted on the executives at NBC, the network responsible for the "Tonight Show." They felt they had a talent on their hands and though they had yet to figure out what they wanted to do with him, they did not want him to get away. So in April 1979—less than a year after Letterman's first appearance on the "Tonight Show"—NBC offered him a two-year contract. The contract did not specify any projects; it simply made Letterman available to the network. By spring of the next year, the NBC executives had decided what they wanted to do with him: star him in his own daytime talk show. On June 23, 1980, one more dream came true for the young comic from Indiana, and the "David Letterman Show" debuted on national television.

With his innate comedic talents and more than 10 years of broadcasting experience, Letterman had certainly earned his new position as host of his own program. But he never forgot Johnny Carson's role in his success. "I don't know of a person in comedy or television who didn't grow up with Johnny Carson as a role model," he once said. In May 1992, one week before Carson retired from "The Tonight Show," he invited Letterman back for a final guest appearance. By this time, Letterman was host of his own popular late-night talk show. Ever grateful to his mentor, he told Carson that night, "Thanks for my career." Letterman, more than anyone else, knew how important that first "Tonight Show" appearance had been.

2 An Unremarkable Childhood

DAVID LETTERMAN WAS BORN the middle child of a middle-class family from the middle of the country. If anything stands out about his childhood, it is how very unspectacular it was. His grandparents on both sides had been coal miners in the eastern part of the United States who had moved to Indiana to become farmers. His mother, Dorothy, was a housewife who became a church secretary, and his father, Joseph, was a florist who owned his own business. The Lettermans lived and worked and sent their children to school in Broad Ripple, a quiet neighborhood of Indianapolis, the state capital. They had a modest home and three children: two girls, Gretchen, the eldest, and Janice, the youngest, and one boy, David Michael, who was born on April 12, 1947.

The grown-up David Letterman has often characterized his upbringing as an American cliché and once described it as "a solid 'Father Knows Best' or 'Leave It to Beaver' type of lower middle-class family," comparing it with the idealized families on 1950s television programs. Of course, no real family is as ideal as those on television, where problems can be solved in a half-hour

Steve Allen (center, wearing chef's hat) directs the television audience in making scrambled eggs on his program the "Steve Allen Show" in 1955. During his high school years, David often stayed up late Friday nights to watch Allen, who originated the "man in the street" broadcasts and who became well known for his hilarious stunts.

time period. The Letterman family had its share of problems, including minding the young David, who, unlike
his sisters, was a smart aleck and something of a trouble-
maker. "I was a maniac," Letterman later said. "From the
time I was six until I was sixteen, there wasn't a peaceful
minute. I was always picking fights, starting trouble. I
don't think there was a single meal where my mother
didn't have to say, 'All right, David. If you can't behave,
take your plate and eat outside.'"

David, who attended elementary school at Public
School 55, just a few blocks from his home, did not enjoy
school and did not do particularly well there. He often
made light of matters his teachers considered important,
though he was never outgoing or boisterous enough to be
called the class clown. He did not like to draw attention
to himself and preferred playing outside with a few
friends, sometimes getting into mischief. Once, when he
was about eight years old, he and his friends brought some
mirrors up into their tree fort, which was located just off
the street. They pointed the mirrors at the sun, and
reflected it into the windshields of cars driving down the
road, temporarily blinding the drivers.

David's mother did not have much tolerance for his
sense of humor. But there were other people in his family
who did, including his grandfather. "My mother's father
was a very funny man—a real smartass, but irresistible.
He'd have me sneak up on watermelons because that was
the only way you could pick them. So there would be this
man in his sixties and me, a little kid, tiptoeing together
through the watermelon patch, and we'd finally grab one
and run like hell." David's father was another one who
"liked to goof off and say funny things and silly things
and do things to provoke you and get under your skin."
Joseph Letterman, according to David, "had a lot of
energy and he had a lot of ideas and a lot of drive, and he
wanted to do things. My mother, by comparison, is the

opposite. She couldn't be more taciturn. Very, very quiet. You want to take her pulse every few minutes. But it was a good combination. He was the circus. He was the show. He was the energy. He was the battery to which all the cables were hooked."

By the late 1950s, when David was not yet a teenager, another source of tension developed in the Letterman household. His father's business began to suffer, and the family felt the financial stress. "We're not talking about poverty or anything dramatic," Letterman later said. "Just the ordinary man's struggle to provide for his family a decent home, clothes that are in style, a summer vacation, and college educations for the kids."

By the time David started high school in 1961, he had developed a strong work ethic and a serious attitude

David attended Broad Ripple High School, seen here in 1961, the year David became a freshman at the school. He had average grades as a student and started to earn a reputation among his buddies as a comic.

toward money, along with a growing sense of humor. The same year he enrolled at Broad Ripple High School, he also started his first job, at the Atlas Supermarket. He had not, however, developed any more interest in his schoolwork, and his grades remained average to poor. Though he began to earn a quiet reputation among his friends as a funny person, he was shy, aloof, and did not call attention to himself. In fact, he felt like an outsider from the many cliques at school, and much of his humor revolved around making fun of those groups. Looking back at this period, Letterman said, "I had two or three friends. We made fun of anything we couldn't do. I was never with the really good-looking kids; and I was never with the really great athletes. But there was always a small pocket of people I hung out with, and all we did was make fun of the really good-looking people and make fun of the really smart kids and make fun of the great athletes."

Plainly put, David did not like school. He was uncomfortable with the social aspects, felt awkward around girls, and was bored with his classes and assignments. Although he loved sports, he could not get excited about the extracurricular activities either. During his first year he played freshman basketball and was a reserve on the freshman track team, but then he quit. He played in the band briefly, and for a little while he joined a club that staged comedy-theater productions. But he did not excel in any of these activities and did not stay with them long. The one endeavor that he stuck with for most of his high school career was his position as hall monitor.

Academically, David remained average and unimpressive. Though he sometimes exhibited a spark of creativity in his schoolwork, it was rarely appreciated by his teachers. Once, for example, he was assigned a composition topic to pick a person and write about an important event in her or his life. The report he turned in was about a man who had committed suicide by swallowing paper towels.

Sid Maurer (seen here in 1995 with his wife), owner of the Atlas Supermarket where David had a part-time job, recalled that Letterman "was always here when I needed him." The supermarket was also the scene of many of David's teenage pranks, including one in which he stuffed real corn husks into a box of cornflakes.

The impression David made on his teachers and school authorities can be summed up in a statement by the school guidance counselor, Marilyn Dearing. Interviewed many years after he graduated, the counselor described David as "a run-of-the-mill ordinary average kid." As for his sense of humor, she said, "I didn't think David was funny then, and I still don't think he's funny."

The Atlas Supermarket, where David worked part-time for four consecutive years, was perhaps as significant to his development as was Broad Ripple High. For David, it was certainly the more enjoyable of the two institutions. The owner of the supermarket, Sid Maurer, enjoyed hiring neighborhood teenagers and looked at them as a kind of extended family. "We're proud of all our kids," Maurer later said. He remembered David as a hard worker who "was always here when I needed him." David started out bagging and carrying out groceries but then worked his way up to stocking shelves, cleaning the store, making deliveries, depositing cash at the bank, and running the cash register.

The Atlas Supermarket also offered David an arena for playing pranks, an activity he soon perfected. He once created a coffee can display by stacking the cans all the way to the ceiling, making it impossible for anyone to buy a can without the whole tower tumbling down. Another time he stuffed a box of cornflakes full of real corn husks and put it on the shelf to be sold. He also liked to make announcements over the loudspeaker for events that were not really going to take place, such as fire drills, a raffle for a new car, or a mah-jongg tournament. The customers dutifully followed each of these announcements, much to the delight of David and at least some of his coworkers.

Aside from his job at the Atlas Supermarket, two things helped David survive high school: his sense of humor and his course in public speaking. As he later explained, "There was a period in high school and maybe that's when it comes for everybody, when you sort of had to figure out who you were. You think, 'Well, I'm not fitting in with this group, the really desirable blue-chip group, and I'm not fitting into that group.' And then you start to examine your own inventory and think, 'Is there anything I can do that is going to make me desirable or make me different?'"

Fortunately for David, he knew he had a skill. "Early on I realized I had this one little tool. I could make people laugh." Unfortunately, he had no idea how to make that tool useful, especially when he considered jobs and careers and other aspects of life after high school. "The problem was, where? How? What am I gonna do? Join the circus?" David's mother shared this concern and was worried about how her son, who was earning C and D grades, was going to find work when he left high school.

"So I took a class in speech and just loved it," he said years later. "For the first time in my formal academic experience there was a subject that seemed to come easily to me, more easily than algebra or geometry or shop. I was not very bright, and may not be very bright in the rest of my life, but at that time it was clear to me that this was something to remember. This was a valuable lesson." The lesson—that he had a talent for the very activity he most enjoyed—was a profound one for David, who was nearing graduation and thinking about his future. "I was not good in math or chemistry and I realized athletics were not going to make me wealthy. The only thing that came easily to me was English—writing and public

This photograph of Letterman appeared in his high school yearbook in 1965, the year he graduated. Letterman recalled later that the high point of his high school years was his involvement in speech class.

speaking. I started to think, 'Is there any way that I can practically apply this to my life?'"

In fact, the ability to speak in front of people, to entertain them and make them laugh, had been a trait that David had admired for many years. The 1950s was the Golden Age of television, when the medium was gaining enormous popularity as a thrilling new media format, and from an early age, David had felt that excitement. When not playing outside, he enjoyed watching a variety of shows, especially comedies. "When I got to an age where I could appreciate comedians, it was guys like Jonathan Winters: he used to really make me laugh hard . . . on Friday nights I could stay up late and watch the 'Steve Allen Show.' And sometimes after school I used to watch 'Who Do You Trust?' with Johnny Carson."

As Letterman later explained, Carson was a particularly attractive figure for him at the time. "When I was a kid, in adolescence, I didn't see much of my father because he was at work all day, working very hard. He owned a flower shop that was not as successful as it could have been, maybe, and it just beat him silly. So when I would get to see 'The Tonight Show' with Johnny Carson, I saw a guy there who looked great, who had a suit on, had a great-looking tie, interviewing beautiful women, smoking a cigarette. . . . I don't want to diminish my father's role in my formative years, but you saw in your father a hard-working guy who was just trying to stay ahead of things. You saw in Johnny Carson—'Oh my God, Jesus, look at this guy.'"

Carson, the suave young comedian from Nebraska who made fun of the contestants on "Who Do You Trust?" may have impressed the young David Letterman as "the model of how cool guys behaved," but it was Steve Allen who affected him most. This multitalented radio and television broadcaster, who was host of the original

"Tonight!" show, was famous for inventing a number of shticks, including remote "man in the street" broadcasts from outside the studio, and stunts such as jumping into a giant vat of Jell-O.

But it was not just comedians who made an impression on the young David. He was also interested in the established broadcasters, the ones who had built careers as radio announcers, like Garry Moore and Arthur Godfrey, and then made the switch to television. Years later, Letterman could still describe the opening of the "Arthur Godfrey Show," which "began with a shot of an empty headset. Big radio headphones dangling from a cord in

Ed Sullivan (center), host of the television variety show the "Ed Sullivan Show," is seen here onstage with clown Emmett Kelly (pointing) and others. Letterman watched Sullivan's popular show every Sunday night—and nearly 20 years after Sullivan's death in 1974, Letterman would tape his own show from the Ed Sullivan Theater in New York City.

29

front of a microphone, everything being as it would normally except that Arthur's head wasn't in the head-phone. I liked the way the headphones and the micro-phone looked. And I thought, 'This stuff looked great.' It made a real impression on me."

Another important television figure during David's youth was Ed Sullivan, whose Sunday-night variety show was for many years the country's most popular. Even David's parents, who did not like to watch much televi-sion, made an exception for the "Ed Sullivan Show." As Letterman recalled, "Every Sunday night at my house we'd have dinner early, and my father would usually make soup that we wished Mom had made. You know it was that kind of soup. 'Oh thanks, Dad.' And then we fin-ished dinner and watched the 'Ed Sullivan Show.'"

It was a great revelation for David to discover that his talent for humor and public speaking coincided with his interest in television and radio. As he explains it, "When I was a kid, I was aware of Arthur Godfrey's daytime show, and Garry Moore, and I found it fascinating to see these people sit at little desks and have these microphones in front of them and talk, and I thought, 'This is amaz-ing,' and I sort of would pretend to be on TV or radio and thought, 'This would be great,' and then I forgot all about it until I got into high school and took a speech class, the first class I didn't have to work too hard to get good grades in." He was shocked and delighted to find out that he excelled at something, and thought to himself, "Wait a minute! I can actually get a grade here, just standing up and telling stories! . . . Now the trick is, how do I find out how to get paid to do this?"

After floundering around as an average student with average grades and not many interests other than fooling around, David had finally found something that excited him. Still, he doubted whether these talents could amount to anything and wondered how they could be applied to a career. When he "found out you could study broadcasting in college, I thought, 'Holy Cow! There you go! It's a miracle! What's next?' And what was next was figuring out how to get on radio." As he eventually discovered, his talent for writing and speaking was not only enjoyable, it was also valuable for a career in broadcasting. Now David knew what he wanted to do and was eager to start working toward it.

In his senior year of high school, he applied to college for the purpose of studying communications and broadcasting. Although he wanted to go to Indiana University at Bloomington, which had one of the best reputations in the state, he knew he was not likely to be accepted because of his poor grades. He also knew that he might have difficulty maintaining the required C average during his freshman year there. So he applied instead to Ball State University, part of the state college system and located in Muncie, about an hour's drive from his home. In September 1965, David Letterman, the average boy from Indianapolis, Indiana, started his college career.

3 Ball State

I N MANY WAYS, the David Letterman who started courses at Ball State University in September 1965 seemed very different from the David Letterman who had graduated from Broad Ripple High School just a few months earlier. He was enthusiastic, dedicated, hardworking, and focused, and he maintained a B average during his first and second years. But his sense of humor and his sense of fun remained the same. The town of Muncie, quiet and rural with a population of about 50,000 at the time, was easy to make fun of and served as a constant source of inspiration for his humor.

Muncie was surrounded by farms, though industry and the university were also key components of the town's economy. The college, which was named for the Ball family, makers of Ball canning jars (who had donated much of their money to start the school in 1918), was originally a school for training teachers. It had just been upgraded to university status a few years before Letterman enrolled. The years that Letterman was in college, 1965 through 1969, were years of great social change and political activity in the United States and many other countries. But Ball State, wrapped like a cocoon in the

In 1966, broadcasting student and disc jockey David Letterman manages the controls of the radio booth at WBST, a campus radio station at Ball State University. He later recalled that "[WBST] was my first outlet, my place to just go and talk, and I loved it."

small town of Muncie, was light years away from the turbulence. "We were amazingly isolated," Letterman recalled. "I was only vaguely aware of the political turmoil of the time."

In 1968, Students for a Democratic Society in Des Moines, Iowa, demonstrate against the Vietnam War. The late 1960s was a period of great political turmoil in the United States, especially on campuses across the nation, where students protested U.S. involvement in the Vietnam War.

During the 1960s, college campuses became important centers for much of the political activity, including the civil rights movement, the peace movement, and the struggle for women's liberation. Across the Pacific, in the small country of Vietnam, U.S. forces joined South Vietnamese troops in fighting against the North Vietnamese. It was a war that many Americans opposed, and antiwar protests broke out all over the country. Columbia University in New York, the University of Cali-

fornia at Berkeley, and the University of Wisconsin at Madison, less than 400 miles from Muncie, were three hubs where students and professors were engaged in teaching, learning about, and acting on social concerns. The peace movement affected many colleges, including Kent State University in Ohio, not far from Muncie, where the National Guard shocked the nation by shooting and killing four students involved in an antiwar demonstration.

The civil rights movement also had campus-based support, including the Student Nonviolent Coordinating Committee (SNCC), begun in 1960. But the movement, which had started years earlier, was broadly based and went far beyond the colleges. Under the leadership of Dr. Martin Luther King, Jr., who advocated a nonviolent approach to bringing about change, the movement gained momentum in the 1960s. However, King was not the only leader working for equality for African Americans. Malcolm X, who for several years belonged to the Nation of Islam, advanced the concept of black power, as did the Black Panthers, a more radical organization. Sometimes the problems of racism, which had been festering in the United States since its early years as a country, erupted into violent outbreaks. The six-day riot in the Watts section of Los Angeles in 1965 and the assassination of Malcolm X that year and Martin Luther King, Jr., in 1968 are just three examples of the racial turmoil that was rocking the nation during this time.

But Ball State "was a lot different from being at Berkeley," according to Letterman. "All I was concerned about was buying a station wagon and getting married." In fact, Letterman said, "I was hardly aware of the Vietnam War until a friend of mine flunked out and was drafted and was dead like *that.* One day, here's a guy setting fire to the housemother's panty hose, and the next day, he's *gone.* That got my attention."

The campus structure pictured here is Ball State University's Fine Arts Building. The university, located in Muncie, Indiana, was isolated from the great social changes occurring in the large urban areas of the country during the late 1960s. Letterman later commented about being a student at Ball State, saying, "I was only vaguely aware of the political turmoil of the time."

Nonetheless, the students at Ball State, including Letterman, were neither very aware nor very interested in the dramatic changes taking place. As Letterman described it, "All over the United States, protest. Kent State was not that far away, and even Bloomington, the campus down there [Bloomington is located south of Muncie], was a hotbed of protest. But not Ball State. We were pretty well protected. Quite honestly, the only protest that I ever was involved in was, we thought we maybe could get the cafeteria cooks to wear hairnets."

What did interest Letterman was getting started in broadcasting, and his first semester he began taking classes in radio and television to complete a major in that department. One of the instructors in the department, Darrell Wible, remembered Letterman as a talented, hardworking student. In an interview, Wible stated, "I had him in several classes starting with mass communication class when he was a freshman in 1966. The class had seventy-five students. He always had the answers to the questions—no comedic stuff—and he was one of only four or five who made an A. . . . After that, he discovered the thrill of being on the air and his scholarly work suffered accordingly."

In one class, described by Letterman biographer Caroline Latham, the final assignment was for each student to produce a half-hour taped radio program. Because the time slots for professional radio and television programs are strict, the students were required to make their programs exactly 30 minutes long, not a second more or less. Letterman's tape demonstrated his affinity for comedy and his interest in exposing the behind-the-scenes aspects of broadcasting. His program, a radio talk show, opened with this introduction: "Hey, kids, close all the windows and turn on the gas. . . . It's the 'Uncle Gimpy Show.'" The show also included a simulated report from a mobile unit that got in a simulated car accident and thus could not complete its report. Several minutes shy of the required length, the show started to end, with background music coming on and Letterman announcing the credits. But just when it seemed that the program was going to end too soon, Letterman as the announcer started yelling, as if speaking to the technician in the control booth. "Will you turn that music down?" he said. For the next few minutes there were shouts between the announcer and the supposed technician, who kept putting the music on too loud, too early, and too fast. Letterman finally got to the end of the closing credits right at the 30-minute mark, thus successfully completing the assignment.

Though Letterman enjoyed his broadcasting classes, his extracurricular activities were in many ways the focus of his college career. As he put it once, "My outside-of-classroom experiences here were valuable." In high school, Letterman had remained indifferent to group activities. But in college, he joined a fraternity, Sigma Chi, and enjoyed living with and playing pranks on his fraternity brothers. One prank, as described by a former Sigma Chi member, was to talk another fraternity member into shaving his head and painting it blue, "so David could point him out as the world's largest ballpoint pen." The main focus of his fraternity life was to have fun, drink beer, stay up late, and play practical jokes. "For some people a fraternity does become a lifelong center of business contacts," Letterman explained later. "They'll call you up in Phoenix and say, 'Well I was a brother and so on, and what do you know about the Henderson account?' It's a big network for businessmen, but I never really fit into that. I mean, I didn't go to homecoming, and I didn't marry the Sweetheart of Sigma Chi." It is not clear how valuable his fraternity activities were, but they certainly kept him entertained.

Another out-of-classroom experience for Letterman was the Dirty Laundry Company, a comedy troupe that he formed with three friends. The other members of the troupe were Ron Pearson, who went on to run an advertising agency in Indianapolis; Joyce DeWitt, who became an actress and costarred in the television series "Three's Company"; and Michelle Cook, a music major who Letterman had begun dating. The Dirty Laundry Company performed original skits and short monologues written by Letterman and the other players. They first performed at a homecoming celebration and then played at campus events as well as private parties and other off-campus affairs. Once, they auditioned (unsuccessfully) for a dinner theater in Indianapolis.

Working with the Dirty Laundry troupe was the first time Letterman had ventured onstage to perform his own comedy. Essentially a shy person, Letterman had for several years been gaining a reputation among his friends as someone who liked to pull off-the-wall pranks and make fun of people. But he always did his joking in informal settings. With the comedy troupe, Letterman seemed to acknowledge that his interest in comedy was serious. He was trying to put his jokes into written form, in monologues and in skits, and he was seeing what it was like to perform comedy in public.

Though Letterman spent time with fraternity activities, classes, the comedy troupe, and his girlfriend, he was devoted to his primary pursuit—a career in broadcasting. On-the-job experience has always been as important as classwork in the broadcasting field, and Letterman quickly got a job at WBST, the campus radio station. With 10 watts of power, WBST was a low-wattage station set up to give students a hands-on opportunity at running a radio station with a limited audience. It was not on the air 24 hours per day, and when it was on, it played mostly classical music. Letterman, who did not especially like classical music, was hired as a disc jockey at the rate of $1.25 per hour. He had a three-hour shift beginning at noon several days per week.

Letterman recounted later, "[WBST] was my first outlet, my first place to just go and talk, and I loved it." Over the years, college radio has gained a reputation for allowing students to clown around and have fun while learning. This was certainly Letterman's attitude, and he began injecting humor into his radio show. One afternoon, according to several Letterman biographers, he introduced the popular "Clair de lune," the third movement of French composer Claude Debussy's *Suite Bergamasque.* In his best parody of a pompous announcer, Letterman said, "You know the de Lune sisters. . . . There was Clair, there was Mabel."

The student manager, who was trying to upgrade the image of the station to make it less amateurish, thought

The WBST studio at Ball State is a low-wattage station that was established to provide students with a hands-on opportunity at running a radio station. Hired as a disc jockey to play classical music, Letterman infused his own sense of humor on the air—until the station manager fired him for what he believed were inappropriate jokes.

Letterman's jokes were inappropriate. But for Letterman, the attempt to make a small college station more professional seemed ludicrous, and he continued his comical manner on the air. After the "de Lune sisters," the manager decided that he had had enough fooling around, and he promptly fired Letterman.

Almost immediately, Letterman got a chance to go on the air again, this time on another campus radio station, WAGO. This station had even less airtime and less power (five watts) than WBST, but it played a mix of popular music. Unlike WBST, which operated in conjunction with the school's communications department, WAGO was a pirate station, not authorized by the university, and was operated with low-grade equipment from a room in a dormitory. Although the station did not have a regular schedule or paid disc jockeys, it did allow Letterman to say whatever he wanted over the air. Soon Letterman had enough experience to land a summer job at a television station back home in Indianapolis, where he worked as a booth announcer.

In 1969, David Letterman and Michelle Cook, who had been dating each other exclusively for several years, got married and moved into an off-campus apartment. In addition to completing their coursework—it was the senior year for both of them—they each took part-time jobs to help pay the rent. Cook found work as a waitress, and Letterman got a job as a substitute announcer at a radio station. This was Letterman's first position at a real radio station, Muncie's WERK, and he was hired to fill in for the regular announcer, a Ball State graduate who was taking a leave of absence. His job was to play records and read the news, which he fulfilled efficiently, professionally, and without much joking.

When the regular announcer came back, Letterman was let go, and he began looking for another broadcasting job. Now married and about to graduate from college, he approached his life with a new seriousness: he spent less time joking around and hanging out socializing and drinking beer. He realized that to make something of himself, he needed to quit drinking and devote himself to his career and to his creative aspirations. Years later Letterman described his thinking at the time: "Four years of drinking in the morning is enough for anybody, unless you're looking at it as a career. Instead, I got a job as a TV announcer in Indianapolis. I had to get there early to sign on, so that was the end of my all-day beer consumption." On the strength of his past performance, he was again able to line up a position for that summer at television station WLWI in Indianapolis.

At the same time, Letterman explored other avenues. Although he enjoyed broadcasting, he had a particular interest in writing and performing television comedy. Though he rarely discussed this interest and kept it a secret from his parents, it had been growing stronger over the years. During his last year in college, he wrote letters to professional broadcasters and other television personalities, seeking advice in establishing a career. One such letter, to Gary Owens, the announcer on television's popular comedy "Laugh-In," came to light in 1993, when Owens found it in a stack of old paperwork. "Dear Mr. Owens," Letterman wrote on Ball State University stationery,

> I am a senior in college and I have spent the last three years in the field of commercial broadcasting, working and studying. While I enjoy, and find challenge in broadcasting, I have come to realize that is only because it gives me an opportunity to use material which I have written myself. I would enjoy a career in radio and television only if it would involve creative writing; more specifically, comedy.
>
> The problem is, however, that I don't know how to get a job as a writer. I have had several occasions to perform

my material successfully, but unfortunately I don't pay myself to write jokes. When I graduate in June, I have a job waiting in Indianapolis with the ABC television affiliate, where I have worked for the last two summers as a booth announcer and weekend weatherman. "Hot Diggity" you may be saying to yourself by now, but I would rather be a writer.

As mentioned above, I am completely ignorant as to what to do to prepare myself for a writing career, or even what to do to secure one. If you have the time, I would greatly appreciate any advice or suggestions you could give. Thank you very much for your time and trouble.

In June 1969, David and Michelle Letterman graduated and prepared for their move to Indianapolis, where David's television job awaited him. By leaving Ball State, Letterman was departing a time and a place where he had undergone great personal maturation. At college he had joined several organizations, solidified his career plans, fallen in love, and married. "Ball State was a place where you could have fun and not get arrested," Letterman later said. "It was a good experience. It was a nice place to grow up . . . radio and TV were perfect for me. A lot of people come to study to be a teacher and then have trouble finding a teaching job. Some study animal husbandry, and there are very few animals that need husbands. But for me it was just practical experience, and I was able to turn it into a career." Over the years, Letterman has remained fond of his alma mater and has consistently made affectionate, and usually comical, remarks about the college.

He has also demonstrated his appreciation by returning to the campus for special events and donating money to the university. Some of his donations have gone toward establishing a scholarship to help pay tuition for students pursuing majors in communications. The scholarship has an interesting stipulation that could best be described as

The plaque that hangs outside the recording studio at Ball State is dedicated to students with a "C" grade average. After Letterman became a celebrity, he established a scholarship to help pay tuition for communications students at the university.

Lettermanesque: only students with a C grade average can qualify. It is awarded to students who show signs of creativity, based on taped samples of their work. Letterman had struggled since primary school to convince his teachers of his abilities, and the stipulations of this scholarship revealed his belief that talents do not always show up on report cards.

Letterman has also donated money to the communications department to help upgrade the video and audio equipment in the recording studio. A plaque hangs outside the studio that bears his signature and this inscription: "Dedicated to all 'C' students before and after me!"

Since he graduated, Letterman's association with Ball State and the town of Muncie has brought fame to both these places, though his comments often poke fun at their provincialism. But, as one Ball State official has remarked, "That's the kind of free publicity that no university could ever afford to buy. It's priceless. Everyone hears the name Ball State."

4 Canned Hams Are Falling

DAVID LETTERMAN, armed with a bachelor of arts degree and a smattering of college broadcasting experience, now set upon his broadcasting career in earnest. Upon graduation, he and his wife, Michelle, moved back to Indianapolis, where David started a summer job as the replacement announcer at television station WLWI-Channel 13. The Lettermans rented a small apartment near the Broad Ripple section where David had grown up, and they rode bicycles until they could afford to buy a car.

According to Letterman, his job duties were easy to master: "Every half hour, I'd give the station's call sign and also announce every public service message." It was not much, but it was a start, and he appreciated it. "Here I was at nineteen, talking to central Indiana. Of course, central Indiana wasn't listening." As summer came to an end, Letterman lobbied the station managers to let him continue working there. The managers decided to keep him on, not as the permanent announcer but as a long-term temporary announcer. "I got that job as a summer vacation relief announcer," Letterman later explained. "And every year they would have auditions to replace me. I went

In 1974, Letterman was hired to host a call-in talk show at WNTS, an Indianapolis radio station. Letterman later recalled, "That was my fantasy: being able to communicate with folks without the unspeakable trauma of having them right there in the same room, scrutinizing me."

through five years of two or three times a week watching them audition my replacement. And—believe it or not—they never found anybody who was even that good!"

He quickly became adept at the relatively simple task of on-air announcements and took advantage of his time at work to observe and learn. Soon, his duties expanded. "I started as a voice-over announcer doing station identifications," he said. "Then gradually, through vacation schedules and attrition, I got to do morning news once, got to host a kids' show once; ended up doing the weather and a late-night movie show. You just do everything you can. It was fun because there was no pressure. I could pretty much do whatever I wanted, and nobody cared because I was always the fill-in guy."

Letterman made the most of these assignments, which he once summed up as "anything that nobody else wanted to do," and he advanced from a being a substitute to hosting shows himself. Fledgling broadcasters at Channel 13 were usually assigned to two programs: a children's 4-H (a farming club) program that aired Saturday afternoons and a late-night movie program that went on at two o'clock in the morning.

When Letterman took over as host of the 4-H show, he named it "Clover Power" and set out to try and make entertaining programming out of interviews with children who had excelled at such 4-H activities as raising prize-winning pigs or growing humongous pumpkins. He was torn between treating the earnest children with a serious professional demeanor and his natural tendency to make jokes about their parochialism. In his comments years later, he described his dilemma: "You'd have a kid with a bad complexion plugging a cord into a socket watching a light bulb light up, and you had to talk to him for ten minutes about it. It was so unnatural, so you had to say, 'I'll be damned, you're kidding, it really lights up like that.'"

On the late-night program, which he called "Freeze-Dried Movies," Letterman was able to cut loose and have more fun on the air. The show, which Letterman later described as "bad, bad, bad Oriental monster movies, sponsored by a place that sold bad, bad, bad Oriental pizza," gave him the leeway to experiment with the techniques and the humor that he had begun to explore in college. "In between the movies, I'd goof around with a cast of regulars. We had a telethon to raise money for a washed-up fighter. We celebrated our tenth anniversary in the show's second week. One guy showed up at the station wearing a stupid suit, and we dragged him onto the show so people could see it." Though the audience at that time of night was sparse, "Freeze-Dried Movies" provided Letterman with an opportunity to forge his own broadcasting style.

But it was as a weekend weather forecaster that Letterman got his greatest exposure. He worked as the substitute, and, according to Letterman, "In the event that harm came to the regular weatherman, I was just a heartbeat away." But even this assignment, with its large audience and its seemingly humdrum subject, presented Letterman with comedic opportunities. "You can only announce the weather, the highs and lows, so many times before you go insane," he said. "In my case it took two weeks. I started clowning. I'd draw peculiar objects on the cloud maps and invent disasters in fictitious cities. I made up my own measurements for hail, and said hailstones the size of canned hams were falling."

Though Letterman was no longer a disc jockey on college radio, he still had some of that same playful attitude, and even the weather seemed to be an endless source of amusement for him. "I used to like to make up cities and circumstances that didn't exist and describe devastation that didn't occur," he said, recalling this period. "I thought that was a high form of entertainment. Looking back on it, it probably wasn't funny, but I enjoyed using television for the purposes of disseminating false data."

It was the very tedium of the weather forecasts that struck Letterman as funny. "Nothing is going to happen to us as far as the weather is concerned," he once announced on the air. "It's going to be just like it was yesterday, and just like it is today, and it's going to be like that tomorrow and again on Tuesday." But the viewers did not always share his sense of humor and sometimes even Letterman admitted that his jokes were less than tasteful. "I remember one night we reported that a tropical storm had just been raised to hurricane status. Well, I was amused at the phraseology and suggested that viewers send postcards to the storm, congratulating it on having made the step up to the major leagues. Of course the next day it killed 8 million people and removed all of South Florida—the most devastating hurricane in years. So I felt a little sorry about that."

Nonetheless, he seemed unable to control himself, and his antics continued. Once, he noticed that the weather map had a mistake in it, and the southern border of Indiana was missing. Letterman took advantage of this error and invited his viewers to "take a look at the cloud cover photograph of the United States made earlier today. I think you'll see that once again we have fallen to the prey of political dirty dealings. And right now you can see what I am talking about. The higher-ups have removed the border between Indiana and Ohio, making it one giant state. Personally, I'm against it." On another occasion of a mapping error, when the state of Georgia was accidentally left off, Letterman claimed that the U.S. government had traded Georgia for the country of Iran, which would soon be inserted in the vacant space. He could find humor in almost anything, including the temperature readings. "Muncie, 42. Anderson, 44," he announced one evening. "Always a close game."

As Letterman became more established at the station and more confident of his on-air style, his joking grew bolder. But viewers who took their weather seriously began to complain to the managers at Channel 13. "People said, 'Who is this punk and why is he making fun of the relative humidity?'" recalled Letterman. As he pointed out once in an interview, "Indianapolis is at the center of an agricultural area where a lot of people depend on the weather for their livelihood." The complaints came in, and Letterman's bosses asked him to tone it down. But he could not help himself. "I just couldn't resist the temptation to just sort of goof around with the weather. . . . I guess it was immaturity more than anything else. It was like goofing off in church—you do it to see what you could get away with."

Though his on-air demeanor was light and joking, Letterman was completely serious about his career. Since his arrival at the station, he had been observing and assessing the various types of positions that existed in the field of television, trying to see where he might fit in. After a few years, he eliminated a few positions that he thought were wrong for him. For instance, "I had no desire to be an anchorman because in the early '70s the idea was that the TV news should be as slick and straight as possible. There was not much an anchorman could do besides read what was on the TelePrompTer [the device that displays the script]." In fact, though his weather forecasts were earning Letterman more complaints than praise, they did provide him with a creative outlet, and he thought that weather announcing might be an avenue for him. "I always thought I'd be the next John Coleman, the likable, funny weatherman who eventually got hired out of the market [the local area]."

In any case, Letterman knew he could not go on forever doing "Clover Power," "Freeze-Dried Movies," and the weekend weather. He was grateful for the opportunities that Channel 13 had given him and once remarked, "It was just great, the best experience anybody could have. It was like graduate school—maybe better." Nonetheless, he felt he had gone as far as he could with the station and he needed to move on. Thinking that a station in a bigger metropolitan area might provide him with more challenges, Letterman began sending inquiries along with videotaped samples of his work to larger-market stations. He received no responses and once surmised the fate of his carefully compiled packets: "They would look at the tape, erase it and keep it in their files to record their weekend sports. I was losing a fortune in videotapes."

After four years at the television station Channel 13 in Indianapolis, Letterman decided to work in radio. The call-in talk show Letterman hosted at WNTS gave him a lot of exposure because it was scheduled for "drive time," when commuters were driving home from work in the late afternoon.

After four years, Letterman decided that there was no more room at Channel 13 for him to advance, creatively or professionally. Although he had not been able to find a job at another television station, he made up his mind to leave Channel 13. In 1974, he landed a position at a local radio station, WNTS, an all-talk station that aired a combination of nationally syndicated programs and locally produced shows.

WNTS hired Letterman to be the host of a call-in talk show, which was scheduled during "drive time," so named because the audience was mostly commuters on their way home from work, who listened on their car radios. Drive time, the late weekday afternoon time slot, is radio's equivalent of television's prime time, the hours between 8:00 and 11:00 P.M. when viewership is highest. It was a time slot that offered Letterman a great deal of exposure.

It also offered him a chance to work in a field—radio broadcasting—that had attracted him since he was a child. According to Letterman, "As a kid I loved the image of Arthur Godfrey doing his radio-TV simulcasts, sitting behind a microphone wearing headphones—just talking." He was especially attracted to radio work because of his shyness in front of people. "That was my fantasy: being able to communicate with folks without the unspeakable trauma of having them right there in the same room, scrutinizing me. . . . When I did local radio and TV in Indianapolis, the thought of appearing live anywhere was just out of the question. People would say, 'Hey Dave, the Kiwanis Club [a national service organization] wants you to come over and kiss their children,' and I'd say, 'No, I can't do that.'" He looked forward to his new radio program with gusto.

But soon after he went on the air, Letterman realized that he was not cut out for this kind of work. He was supposed to discuss politics and current events, topics in which he had very little interest, and be personable and friendly with anyone who called his program. According to Jeff Smulyan, who also worked at WNTS, "The average listener was probably 50 years old. They'd call up and say, 'Hey Dave, there are Communists in Carmel.' And Dave would say, 'Well, give them Carmel, ya know? The schools are overcrowded, and the zoning laws are too restrictive.'" Once again, Letterman was unable to take his audience seriously, and he began making fun of them. He later said, "I talked to morons on the telephone—people who had found a way to make tires out of cheese; folks who could prove that someone was building a giant brain magnet on Neptune." Just as he had done on the weekend weather, Letterman began introducing comedy to his show under the guise of news and information. Once he announced that the Soldier's Monument, a locally famous 230-foot statue in the center of Indianapolis, was being replaced with a miniature golf course. The statue, he said, had been sold to Guam, where it would be painted green, just like their national vegetable, the asparagus.

Letterman, who had always been a sports fan, also liked to invent fictional sporting events and describe them on the air. One such sport involved a ball eight feet in diameter that one team would try to maneuver off the playing field and onto the opposing team's bus. He also made up stories about the event for which Indianapolis is most famous—the Indianapolis 500 auto race. Every year, in the weeks before the race, excitement takes hold of the city, and the news media is full of Indy 500 stories. Letterman took advantage of this excitement and, in the days leading up to the race, made an announcement over the air about a supposed rift among the race organizers. One faction was breaking away, he declared, and starting another race on Interstate 70, which connected Indianapolis to Kansas City. He admonished his listeners to be

Letterman was inspired by radio and television personality Arthur Godfrey. "As a kid," Letterman explained, "I loved the image of Arthur Godfrey doing his radio-TV simulcasts, sitting behind a microphone wearing headphones—just talking."

careful of the racing cars while driving on that highway, then opened up the phone lines to concerned, confused callers.

Letterman continued to display his interest in exposing the seams of broadcasting by talking about the behind-the-scenes producers and technicians who worked alongside him at the station, sometimes sticking a microphone in front of them and making them talk, impromptu, on the live airwaves. Another series of pranks involved spreading false rumors about local celebrities. Jane Pauley, a local broadcaster who went on to great national success on the "Today" show, grew up in Indianapolis not far from Broad Ripple. In 1974, she was a television newscaster at Indianapolis's Channel 8, and Letterman, bored with the tedium of his radio show callers, once announced that she was getting married and urged his listeners to send her cards and presents. Years later, Letterman described his attitude toward his show: "I was doing the kind of radio talk show where you get the guy from the Elbow Foundation or the woman who has 167 fig recipes and I just didn't care anymore. So I'd

Jane Pauley, an Indianapolis newscaster when Letterman first met her, later went on to national fame on the "Today Show." In 1974, Letterman announced on his call-in radio show that Pauley was getting married and urged listeners to send her cards and gifts. The announcement was one of his many pranks to confuse callers.

announce that Jane had been married and wait for her to call up seething."

Though the radio show gave him plenty of space for joking, Letterman hated it. He later said, "I was miscast because you have to have somebody who is fairly knowledgeable, fairly glib, possessing a natural interest in a number of topics. That certainly is not me: I don't care about politics; I don't care about the world economy; I don't care about martians cleaning our teeth."

In June 1972, members of the Republican Committee to Re-elect the President had engaged in numerous illegal activities to ensure that President Richard Nixon would win the election. They hired burglars to break into the Democratic National Committee's headquarters in the Watergate office complex in Washington, D.C., to search for useful material and records. As it unfolded, the scandal—known as Watergate—soon implicated the president himself. A congressional investigation revealed that President Nixon had not only been aware of the break-in but had actually approved it. The investigation also revealed that he then abused the powers of his office to thwart the investigation into the break-in and the Republican committee's cover-up. Eventually, as the threat of Nixon's impeachment grew strong, the president stepped down from office, resigning in August 1974 in shame and embarrassment.

While the country got caught up in these historic events, Letterman remained as aloof toward politics as he had always been. "The Nixon-Watergate nonsense was the perfect example of something about which I knew nothing and couldn't have cared less . . . all these political mavens would call wanting to discuss the intricacies of the left and the right and what did I know? I was just your average jerk, so I didn't do them much good. I did it for a year and literally thought I would lose my mind."

In fact, it was less than a year before Letterman began looking for another job. He had already tried to find work at television stations all over the country, so now he looked once again at the opportunities around him. The way Letterman saw it, "I could have become one of any number of guys who have stayed on in any market in the country. There are guys who have been on twenty-five years; they become Fred Heckmans [a successful local broadcaster], they become the dean of this and the dean of that, and they speak at the Rotary club and the next thing you know they're dead." To Letterman, these prospects were dismal. His only option, he felt, was to move. As one of his colleagues at WNTS expressed it, "Dave had a talent that was bigger than the city of Indianapolis."

Letterman had already tried several formats, in both radio and television, but none of them seemed quite right for him. He enjoyed being funny and wanted to find work that would welcome, not spurn, this interest. Hoping to break into television comedy, he began writing scripts while still at his job with WNTS radio. He wrote scripts for network programs, such as the popular comedies the "Mary Tyler Moore Show" and the "Bob Newhart Show," hoping that they would provide him with an entry into the next level of television.

For the five years since he had graduated from college, Letterman's life had consisted mainly of his work. He and Michelle had friends, and they socialized somewhat, but

Letterman preferred to spend time alone with his wife or to work on his own projects. Michelle Letterman was very supportive of David's aspirations; she felt he had the talents to succeed nationally and did what she could to encourage him. In 1974, Letterman's father died, and soon after, David and Michelle Letterman began toying seriously with the idea of moving to Los Angeles, the hub of the television industry.

It was not an easy decision to make, and Letterman agonized over it. "I was too unhappy with myself to stay in Indianapolis. If you're secure with yourself, then regardless of where you are, you're happy and you lead a productive life, and have kids and go to Rotary meetings and you have, you know, a great life. But if you're

Ed Asner, as Lou Grant, and Mary Tyler Moore, as Mary Richards, appear in a 1977 episode of the "Mary Tyler Moore Show." Around 1975, Letterman wrote television scripts for popular network comedies, including the "Mary Tyler Moore Show," hoping to land a permanent job as a TV scriptwriter.

insecure like me and millions of other young airheads, you move to Los Angeles and entertain drunks in bars. Or try to." What Letterman wanted was to try to make it at the network level of television, to work on comedy shows as a writer and perhaps as a performer.

But his ties to the quiet, conservative Midwest were strong, as was his fear of failure. He was a hardworking, frugal young man who, aside from his tendency to make jokes when people thought he should not, had a serious attitude toward his work. His options in Indianapolis were not grand, but they were secure. Still, he sometimes thought he might have what it took to make it on the national level. Michelle Letterman, on the other hand, was sure that David had what it took. She had been around him and his sense of humor for years, and she knew it was time to move to Los Angeles. In the end, as Letterman later explained, "I went to Los Angeles because I had done everything in local broadcasting that I could and I still wasn't getting hired out of the market. . . . I'd watch network TV and think, 'Jeez, I'm at least that funny,' so I wrote a bunch of scripts and went to L.A." While David agonized over the decision to leave Indiana, Michelle tried to convince him that it was the right thing to do. Several times he made up his mind to move, only to back out of his decision. But finally Michelle won out. "She started running around packing the dishes and telling me this time we were really going to do it," he said later. "She was very supportive. I knew I was going to fail."

5 The Big Time: Los Angeles

ON MEMORIAL DAY WEEKEND 1975, David and Michelle Letterman packed their belongings, including David's comedy scripts, into their red pickup truck and headed west. Letterman, a pragmatist who did not like taking risks, was still convinced it was the most foolish thing he had ever done.

"We loaded everything we owned into a pickup truck and drove cross country, just quit our jobs and moved. And my parents—my father was dead by that time, but my mother, God bless her, never said a thing. I said, 'Mom, I'm moving to California.' She never said, 'Why? What are you, nuts? What the hell are you going to do?' Never. And I can remember her, with my two sisters, standing on the lawn of my house—we just drove by to say goodbye to them, and she never questioned it, just said, 'Okay, bye.'"

It was not until years later that he would be able to look back on his move to Los Angeles as a positive step. "Ultimately, it wasn't so much a matter of bravery. You keep conditioning yourself in risk situations. 'Well, if it all explodes in my face, I can always come back to Indianapolis and get work.' So I convinced myself by looking at the other side of the argument that I

In 1978, Letterman landed a job on Mary Tyler Moore's comedy variety show on television. Letterman was hired as a contributing writer and as a cast member. Critics panned the show, however, and after three weeks, it was canceled.

really had nothing to lose. You sort of trick yourself into thinking that it's an extended vacation or a high adventure. But the truth of the matter was I felt pretty foolish giving up a job that was making good money for me. Driving across the country that May, I felt pretty stupid."

When they arrived in Los Angeles, the Lettermans stayed at a motel while they looked for a place to live. Once they found an apartment, they began looking for work. Michelle landed a job almost immediately as a buyer for Mays department store. Meanwhile, Letterman was trying to find a way to break into the television business by bringing his scripts to producers at various television studios, in the hopes that someone would either buy one or hire him to write for comedy shows. Unfortunately, there were (and still are) floods of aspiring writers trying to sell scripts and get hired to write for programs. Letterman's scripts, much like the videotapes he had earlier sent to television stations, went unnoticed.

This was his first sobering lesson about the television industry. "I told everyone, including myself, that I was going out there to become a TV scriptwriter. I thought that would be my best entry point into the business. But the thing you discover is that you can write all the scripts you want when you're living in Indianapolis. People are not going to meet you at the L.A. city line saying, 'Can we see those scripts? We're dying to get scripts from people who live in Indianapolis.' It just doesn't work that way. I'd take my scripts around and they'd toss them into a warehouse, and every Thursday, the guy with the fork-lift would go by, pick up all the scripts and bury them near the river."

At the same time, Letterman was trying another approach to getting work in television. Before leaving Indianapolis, he had collected a few names of people in Los Angeles that might be able to help him, and he now began to contact these people. He tried to reach a talent agent who had been recommended to him, but the agent had gone out of business. So he pursued a second lead and called Betty White and Allen Ludden, whom he had met while they were on a promotional visit in Indianapolis. White and Ludden, stars of several network programs, arranged for Letterman to be a panelist on their latest show, a comedy quiz show called "What Is It?" Letterman went on the show, which required him to humorously identify a series of unusual-looking objects. But this lead, which had seemed promising, was also a dead end, and nothing more came out of it.

Part of Letterman's difficulties in finding work were demographic. Since the early part of the century, when the movie studios first moved to Los Angeles to take advantage of the warm climate and the lenient industry regulations, the city had become a mecca for those aspiring to work in the entertainment business. Because of the sheer numbers of people and the fierce competition among them, only a small percentage of the hopeful actors, writers, directors, and producers ever find work in "the business." For many of those who do succeed, it takes years of persistence, patience, and hard work. But Letterman, who could be persistent, and certainly worked hard, was easily discouraged. After several weeks of leads that went nowhere, he grew impatient and frustrated. "I panicked," he later admitted. "It was the first time in my adult life that I didn't have a real job."

Nonetheless, he persevered. Soon after Letterman arrived in Los Angeles, he tried another approach to breaking into the comedy business. He went to the Comedy Store, a nightclub that featured both established and aspiring comedians, and watched the performances. One night each week the club sponsored an "open mike" night, which allowed amateurs to try out their routines in front of an audience. Though he hated to perform in front of people, Letterman decided to give it a try because

Comedian Steve Martin gives the raspberry during a performance (in which he pretends to be a caveman building a fire with imaginary dung) at the Comedy Store nightclub in Los Angeles, California, in 1978. After moving to Los Angeles, Letterman tried to break into the comedy business at the popular Comedy Store, and over time he was able to perfect the delivery of his jokes.

the Comedy Store was such good exposure. Producers and talent scouts came often to the club looking for new performers—Robin Williams, Steve Martin, and Jay Leno are just three of the comics who worked at the Comedy Store before going on to great popularity. Most comedians worked at other, less prominent clubs before braving the stage at the Comedy Store. But Letterman, with no experience, went straight to the hub. According to Letterman, "I'd never performed as a stand-up comedian before, partly because there's just no place to do that in Indianapolis or Ball State. Oh, you can do it in your home, but it gets little response."

So Letterman wrote down a batch of jokes, memorized them, and went to the club on open mike night, where he mounted the stage and recited his jokes. The audience response? "Dead silence," according to Letterman. He later described the experience: "The first time, I found it very painful to get up in front of those people. And I wasn't exactly a big hit either. . . . I remember thinking, 'Jeez, I've come 2,500 miles and gotten onstage in this dimly lit bar in front of these mutants, and I'm telling jokes.'"

Worse than the pain of performing, however, was Letterman's conviction that he had failed. With this poor performance, Letterman thought, his chances of getting work in television comedy were reduced even further. Years later, he shared these feelings: "When you go out there and you have something that you think is funny, it's such a personal little presentation. It's you trying to make a roomful of people laugh or a whole country of people laugh, and if they don't laugh, it's just like you've been embarrassed in your third-grade class and your teacher has reprimanded you. It's the worst sinking feeling in the world, it's the deepest embarrassment you can endure. Here you are showing off, and nobody thinks you're funny."

Either Letterman's debut at the Comedy Store was not as bad as he thought, or his determination got the best of him. He wrote more jokes and worked on his delivery. He also spent many nights at the club, observing other comics. Watching Jay Leno, who had been doing stand-up comedy for years, was particularly instructive. According to Letterman, when he saw Leno's act, "I thought, 'Aww, I see, *that's* how it's supposed to be done.' It wasn't two guys go into a bar, and it wasn't bathroom jokes. It was smart, shrewd observations, and it could be anything—politics, television, education. The dynamic of it was, you and I both understand that this is stupid. We're Jay's hip friends." For Letterman, who knew he could be funny but never thought of himself as a comic, Leno offered an example of how he could turn his attitude and the way he saw things into an act. Both Leno and Letterman shared an affinity for looking at the absurdities of everyday life and tended to stay away from blue, or sexual, humor. But Letterman was offbeat, edgier, more sharply sarcastic, and he usually stayed away from the subject of politics.

Soon he was back at the Comedy Store with a new repertoire of jokes, a better delivery style, and a more confident stage presence. Although he still did not enjoy performing, he was getting better at it. In fact, he got good enough to graduate from amateur status to become a paid performer. Soon he was appearing at the club regularly; for the first time, he was earning an income by being funny.

Working at the Comedy Store also gave Letterman the opportunity to develop a comedic style, which he once described as "not so much jokes as [it is] sarcastic comments, expressions of an attitude." Letterman has also used the term "observational comic" to describe himself, and many others have called his style one of "found humor." In summing up his style, Letterman has said: "What I look for are the setups in life, and then I fill in the punchlines. Like one of my favorite jokes came right out of *National Enquirer,* which every week gives you a million setups. I'm standing there buying cantaloupes, and there's this headline in the *Enquirer* that says, 'How to Lose Weight Without Diet or Exercise.' So I think to myself, 'That leaves disease.' I've been doing that word for word for four years, and it never fails to get laughs."

For new comedians like Letterman, the Comedy Store offered great visibility and great potential for leading to more opportunities. Shortly after he had become a paid performer, Letterman was contacted by Jimmie Walker, a comic actor who was then starring in "Good Times," a popular television comedy. Walker had enjoyed Letterman's act and wanted to hire him to write jokes. Letterman thought he was an odd choice for Walker because "he wanted me to write jokes with a black point of view. Which was interesting, because he was the first black person I had ever seen. . . . Who better to capsulize the American black experience than a white guy from Indiana?" But at a rate of $150 per week for 15 jokes, Letterman did not complain. He was very appreciative for the vote of confidence, as well as for the income, and years later said that he will "always be grateful to Jimmie for that early support."

But Walker was only one of the contacts Letterman made at the Comedy Store. At the beginning of 1977, Jack Rollins, a talent manager with a reputable Los Angeles agency, was impressed enough with Letterman's act to sign him on as a client. He thought Letterman demonstrated an instinctive talent but was still a bit rough. As Rollins later commented, "His standup was okay, but if there was anybody right for television, it was Dave. He's a guy who grew up with TV, he cut his eye teeth on it and he is a Midwesterner. That seems to give him this universal appeal." Through his agent, Letterman got jobs writing jokes for comedians Bob Hope and Paul Lynde and for country music singer John Denver, who was then host of a television variety show. Rollins also booked him to perform on several minor television shows, including the "Gong Show," a game show that encouraged crudeness; the "Peeping Times," a news parody; and two music-variety shows, "Don Kirschner's Rock Concert" and the "Starland Vocal Band Show."

But the most encouraging contact Letterman made through the Comedy Club was with representatives of the "Tonight Show." Though the talent scouts did not think Letterman was polished enough to appear on the show, they did approach and let him know they were watching him. For Letterman, just the fact that they had noticed him was a thrill, and he continued to improve his stand-up routine, hoping one day to make it to the "Tonight Show."

Though his career was advancing at a steady clip, all was not well for David Letterman. Los Angeles and the world of show business were very different from Muncie and Indianapolis, and Michelle and David Letterman began to experience difficulties in their marriage. Initially, it seemed that the problem was one of schedules, as David's jobs generally started at night, just as Michelle was coming home from her nine-to-five position at the department store. "At night she would come home and I would go out," Letterman later explained. "We started not seeing each other week in and week out." But the marital problems proved to be more serious and more fundamental than the issue of work schedules. Letterman once summed it up by saying, "Our basic problem was that we'd just gotten married too young." It was, he said, "a common mistake. You're just looking to Take A Step Into Something to get away from being a kid."

The Lettermans divorced in 1977. It was an emotional strain for both Michelle and David, who had initiated the divorce. As he later said, "I was really committed and I couldn't believe it when it came to an end." Michelle had been Letterman's most loyal supporter and for nine years of marriage she had encouraged him to believe in his talents and pursue his ambitions. It was Michelle who insisted on moving to Los Angeles when David was ready to back out. In later years, Letterman commented on the value of his wife's support and acknowledged his guilty feelings for divorcing her. Nonetheless, the marriage was failing both of them, and he needed to end it.

Though his personal life was turbulent, Letterman's career continued to progress smoothly. In the summer of 1978, in an odd twist of fate, he landed a job on a new television program, the "Mary Tyler Moore Hour," starring none other than Mary Tyler Moore, whose previous show had inspired Letterman to write several scripts. Moore's company, MTM Enterprises, and her producer and husband, Grant Tinker, had solid reputations in television, and the new variety show was Letterman's first spot on a show of some quality. He was hired to fill two positions: contributing writer and cast member. The chance to be a part of the writing team, coming up with jokes and creating skits, filled him with excitement. Being a comedy writer for television shows had been a dream of his since college.

But his performing duties filled him with dread. Letterman had worked long and hard to get to the point where he could get up in front of a live audience and deliver jokes in his stand-up routine. But he was even less comfortable in the role of an actor. His background was in broadcasting, and he had neither the training nor the interest in playing in skits. Singing and dancing in costume was exactly what Letterman did not want to be doing in television and he felt "just mortified. I was like a spring that was coiling ever more tightly."

His job on Moore's program "was the best experience and the worst experience I had had," according to Letterman. He added:

> I was living in one room on Sunset Boulevard, driving a '73 pickup truck. I'd get in my truck and drive to work everyday—which was Television City. In Hollywood! And one of my coworkers was Mary Tyler Moore! It was great, the American show-biz dream come true. It was also difficult because in each show there was a big dance number, and every Tuesday the wardrobe people would come around and fit you for, like, a Peter Pan suit to wear in the number. I always described it as: What's wrong with this picture? Well, Letterman has no business being there with Mary Tyler Moore, that's what's wrong with this picture.

In October 1978, Letterman races a kayak during a television program called "Battle of the Network Stars," which took place in Malibu, California. One month later, Letterman made his fateful appearance on Johnny Carson's "Tonight Show."

Nonetheless, it was work, and it was on network television. Despite his complaints, it was still "pretty exciting, having heard about Television City all my life, to be going to work there. I had a name badge with a picture on it and an ID number, and I could eat in the CBS commissary. I could talk to Mary Tyler Moore anytime I wanted. I could do almost anything. I could share fruit with her if I wanted to. I, of course, wanted to."

Moore's show debuted on September 24, 1978. Panned by critics and audiences alike, it was canceled just three weeks later. In that short period, however, the show had benefited Letterman in several ways. It had provided him with prime-time exposure on national television and a good lesson in working and performing at that level.

His work on the show was noticed by the scouts for the "Tonight Show," who felt he had improved a great deal from the last time they saw him at the Comedy Store. They soon approached Letterman and invited him on the show. On November 26, 1978, Letterman appeared on the "Tonight Show," delivered a polished routine, and chatted with host Johnny Carson. It was the single most important performance of his life, and it changed the direction of his career.

Moore's show had also provided Letterman with a more personal benefit: it gave him the opportunity to work with a friend of his from the Comedy Store, comedy writer Merrill Markoe. Markoe and Letterman had started dating each other and then, by coincidence, they each got a job on Moore's program. Markoe, who had a graduate degree in fine arts from the University of California at Berkeley (one of the campuses that *had* been involved in the political and social movements of the times), taught art before pursuing comedy writing and performing. She, too, enjoyed writing more than performing, and she especially enjoyed writing for Letterman. They worked well together, both personally and professionally, despite the differences in their backgrounds. "She's verbal and uncompromising about what's worth pursuing," Letterman once said. "She's intelligent. Nothing like I am." But as Markoe explained, "We're both intense, neurotic people who worry about everything and expect the worst."

Comedian Robin Williams (right), who had often performed at the Comedy Store, plays Mork on the television series "Mork and Mindy." In the late 1970s, Letterman made guest appearances on several programs, including "Mork and Mindy."

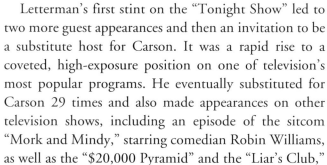

Letterman and Merrill Markoe, a comedy writer, attend a party in 1979. Markoe and Letterman dated and eventually worked and lived together. She once commented, "We're both intense, neurotic people who worry about everything and expect the worst."

Letterman's first stint on the "Tonight Show" led to two more guest appearances and then an invitation to be a substitute host for Carson. It was a rapid rise to a coveted, high-exposure position on one of television's most popular programs. He eventually substituted for Carson 29 times and also made appearances on other television shows, including an episode of the sitcom "Mork and Mindy," starring comedian Robin Williams, as well as the "$20,000 Pyramid" and the "Liar's Club,"

two game shows that billed him as a celebrity contestant. Then, in April 1979, less than a year after his first "Tonight Show" appearance, NBC executives offered Letterman a contract with the network. The two-year contract paid Letterman approximately $350,000 per year but did not specify what he was to do to earn this salary. The network was putting him on retainer—paying him to remain available for whenever the development team came up with a job for him.

Letterman found his new circumstances baffling. Being called a celebrity was amusing, but his new contract seemed too good to believe. In an interview that year, he said, "I keep waiting for someone to tap me on the shoulder and say, 'Okay, buddy, give us the money back, NBC wants your new home, and you have to go back to Indianapolis.'"

In 1979, Markoe and Letterman did go to Indianapolis, but just for a visit. It was his first time back since he had moved to Los Angeles. "I didn't go home for nearly four years," he explained later. "I felt embarrassed because I had not accomplished anything, plus I had just gotten a divorce—it was awkward to come home."

By 1979, Letterman must have felt somewhat accomplished, because he said yes to an invitation from Ball State to appear at the university's homecoming celebration. He had, after all, become a stand-up comedian, a television comedy writer, and a substitute host for Johnny Carson. He also had an agent, a contract with a television network, and a new home near Malibu, California. Markoe, who accompanied him to Indiana, was amused to see Letterman treated like a celebrity everywhere he went. In Muncie, he gave advice to students on how to make a career in show business. In Indianapolis, he appeared in local commercials produced by his friend from college, Ron Pearson. Markoe, every bit as sarcastic as Letterman, said the visit taught her "what it would be like to have been married to one of the Beatles."

Four years earlier, Letterman had left Indianapolis in trepidation, fearing that he was making a foolish mistake. But his perspective had changed during his time in Los Angeles, and he was sure he had done the right thing. "There really was no risk in my case," he said. "It was an imaginary risk. I always wondered why I couldn't get out of the city. I wondered why I couldn't get another job. And then when I just left and found myself succeeding by the definition of my peers, then I realized that Jeez, if you want to do something, then you can certainly do it by just going to work on it. That was a real revelation for me."

"The David
6 Letterman
Show"

OVER THE YEARS, entertainment journalists had made a hobby out of speculating who would ascend to the throne when the King of the Night stepped down. No one knew when Johnny Carson would decide to retire, but over the years he had made several threats to do so. When word of Letterman's NBC contract hit the news media, it sparked a new set of rumors that the network was grooming Letterman to be the next host of the "Tonight Show." Letterman's close association with the "Tonight Show"—he had launched his career on the program and then became a frequent substitute host—seemed proof enough for reporters to start referring to Letterman as the probable replacement for Carson.

The speculations and the comparisons to Carson both flattered and unsettled Letterman. He had admired Carson since he was a child, and it made him feel uncomfortable to be discussed alongside one of his idols. Whenever the issue arose, he deferred and instead praised Carson's achievements. Though he had long dreamed about succeeding Carson, he kept quiet about this desire and was either too polite or too cautious to talk

In May 1980, Letterman is photographed in New York City, one month before his live daytime talk show is to be telecast from the NBC Studios. The program would include permanent cast members, featured guests, interviews with nonpublic figures, musicians, and Letterman's interaction with the audience.

Johnny Carson, as Floyd R. Turbo, a man of many opinions, comments on an issue during the "Tonight Show Starring Johnny Carson" in 1979. That year, rumors began to circulate about Carson's retirement and who might replace him as host of the "Tonight Show."

about replacing Carson before Carson had stepped down. As he said at the time, "It's exciting to guest-host, but not as exciting as doing the show *with* Carson. . . . He's the best straight man in the business."

Another reason why Letterman may have avoided talk of taking over the "Tonight Show" is that his feelings on the subject were mixed. On the one hand, "The association for me with the show has been good. For comedians, it's a real stamp of approval, and it's reflected in the money you make on the outside. I like doing the show and the people are supportive." But on the other hand, "I can never fully relax because it's not my own show. You're driving someone else's car and wearing someone else's underwear. Carson has made it everything there is, so the best you can hope for is to be favorably compared to him."

It was not just the daunting figure of Carson that Letterman feared; it was the show itself, which had endured in its current format for almost three decades. Much as he admired Carson, Letterman had his own ideas for running a talk show, and he doubted that he could be satisfied with someone else's show. As he explained, "One night I was sitting in Carson's chair and I said to myself, 'Well, wait a minute. I am not doing anything different. I am just being Johnny Carson.' I knew that to make my mark in the world I had to do more of what I wanted to do."

As it turned out, Carson was not going to step down anytime soon, so the rumors remained at the speculation stage and Letterman did not have to make any definitive statements. NBC's executives soon began discussions with him to develop his own program. Their first proposal was an afternoon program to be called "Leave It to Dave." Letterman later described this idea as "a disaster from word one. . . . I was supposed to sit on a throne, and the set was all pyramids. The walls were all covered in shag carpet. It was like some odd Egyptian theme sale at Carpeteria." The project never materialized.

But the next proposal, for a morning talk show, seemed more appropriate. Unlike slipping into somebody else's shoes (or underwear) on an established show, Letterman would be creating his own talk show, broadcast live from the NBC studios in New York City's Rockefeller Center. He and Markoe, who was hired as the head writer, were brimming with ideas for the new show and eager to start working on it. They flew to Manhattan, found an apartment, and began preparations for an early summer airdate.

Just four days before the premiere of "The David Letterman Show," the producer and the associate producer left the show. News reports said they left because of "a power struggle with comedian Letterman." But the disagreements between Letterman and these producers were not the only behind-the-scenes problems on the new show. The NBC executives had their own ideas about its style and content, ideas that clashed with Letterman's. The show was scheduled to air weekdays in the middle of the morning, a time slot with an audience made up mostly of women who work at home. NBC executives were pushing for the type of program that had proved successful with this audience: an informative, entertaining show with light news, cooking demonstrations, and celebrity guests. This was exactly the kind of show that Letterman and Markoe did not want to do. They were interested primarily in comedy.

Despite all these problems, the staff of the "David Letterman Show" forged ahead, fueled mainly by the enthusiasm of Letterman and Markoe, who had taken over as producer while still maintaining her position as head writer. The show premiered on June 23, 1980, with Letterman introducing himself as someone who had guest hosted the "Tonight Show," and then adding, "But let's face it—who hasn't?" He then chatted with several people in the audience, sent one of them out for coffee, and, not even midway through the program, he brought on a television critic, who gave his opinion of the show up to that point. From the very beginning, it was clear that this show had little in common with other daytime programs.

The first show left Letterman and Markoe exhausted and not sure how they were going to come up with 90 minutes of comedy and entertainment on a daily basis. According to Letterman, "The show was running us. Actually, it was chasing us down the street. But NBC told us not to worry. They said, 'You have twenty-six weeks; let it evolve.'"

What the show evolved into was a haphazard combination of celebrity interviews, appearances by a cast of actors playing comical guests, music from a house band, brief news updates by a newscaster, and daily reports from bus terminals around the country from a correspondent who was traveling by Greyhound. Letterman orchestrated it all, his wisecracking sarcasm pervading every aspect of the program. He summed up his new show by explaining, "It's my show, but one person can't fill it up.

I think people will watch it for its elements. What will prevail is my attitude—not necessarily my on-camera attitude. And my attitude is pretty much that nothing should be taken all that seriously." That attitude was also prominent in two features invented by Markoe: stupid pet tricks and the pretaped remote segments that were filmed outside the studio. Bob and Stan, the German shepherds owned by Letterman and Markoe, were the inspiration for stupid pet tricks, a spectacle in which pets and their owners came onto the show to demonstrate odd, sometimes ridiculous stunts. Stupid pet tricks has gone on to become a standard Letterman shtick. "When I'm dead people will be doing that on the moon," he said in a 1995 interview with CNN talk-show host Larry King.

The remote segments pitted the midwestern "gee-whiz" persona of Letterman against the hardened urban environs of New York City. These segments, which gave Letterman a chance to show off his prowess at ad-libbing, also gave him a showcase for one of his longtime interests—revealing the usually invisible workings of the television medium. As Markoe later explained, "Dave always wanted to go outside the studio. And it started out pretty easy. I had a big backlog of stuff that went by either geography or theme. We'd go down to Chinatown and tie everything together that I could write a joke into, or else we'd take a tour. One time we went to everything that had the sign WORLD'S BEST COFFEE."

In the television business, a program's popularity is measured by a ratings system devised by the A. C. Nielsen Company. The Nielsen ratings are determined by surveys conducted independently of the networks.

Letterman and NBC executives disagreed about the content of his daytime show: NBC wanted a show that contained the news, cooking demonstrations, and celebrities, whereas Letterman wanted strictly comedy.

They indicate the average audience size as well as the percentage of total viewers that are watching each program. A program's ratings are its pulse, and executives rely on them to determine the health of their shows. Networks make money by selling advertising, and the higher the ratings of a show, the more money the network can charge for running commercials during that show.

The initial ratings for the "David Letterman Show" were very poor: it came in last place of all the programs in its time slot and was watched by only 11 percent of the households that were watching television at that time. The critics did not like the show much either, and most reviews in the press panned it.

"In the first week, you could hear the affiliates mailing in their cancellations," said Letterman, describing the public's unfavorable response to his show. Affiliates are the local branch stations of the national networks, so called because they are affiliated with, though not controlled by, one of the networks. From the 1950s until 1987, when Fox joined the fray, there were three networks—NBC, CBS, and ABC. The affiliate stations in each market area tailor their programming to their particular area and broadcast a combination of network-produced and locally produced programs (such as the local news show that Letterman worked on at Indianapolis's ABC affiliate). Shortly after the "David Letterman Show" went on the air, many stations decided to return to their former, more popular midmorning program. Letterman, a veteran of affiliate broadcasting, could see that his show was in trouble. "We had no problem with NBC till Boston announced that they were dropping out," he said. "Then it went like a wave. Philadelphia, Detroit, and San Francisco went. The other shoe had dropped. We lost two dozen cities in a matter of weeks."

Letterman and his staff, in conjunction with the network executives, worked on improving the show. There

Merrill Markoe took over as producer of Letterman's show, while also serving as head writer. Markoe devised the stupid pet tricks and the pretaped remote segments that were filmed outdoors for the show.

were staff changes, including a new director who had a strong talk-show background and a new producer who took over some of Markoe's responsibilities, allowing Markoe to concentrate on writing. The set, which had been criticized in the press, was redesigned, and the running time of the program was cut to one hour, making it more manageable to produce.

But nothing seemed to help the ratings, and the pulse of the "David Letterman Show" grew dimmer and dimmer. Though NBC had initially scheduled the show for a six-month run, Letterman knew that with such low ratings it could be canceled at any time. At first, he and his staff were discouraged by the news that their show was a flop. But then, as Letterman later explained, they had a curious change of attitude. "Every day, while we were struggling to put the show together, there'd be a story in the paper foretelling our doom. It eventually got to be fun. We created a kind of bunker mentality, trying to do as many unusual things as possible before the end came." Though he felt abandoned by the network and disheartened by the ratings, he forged ahead, guided by this philosophy: "We've got nothing to lose. We're sinking. Let's do whatever we want to do."

Instead of running and hiding from the poor ratings, Letterman and his team ran toward them and embraced them. Those few viewers that did tune in were treated to an energetic series of shows filled with a zany, reckless humor rarely found on television, especially daytime television. In a "Cancellation Sweepstakes," Letterman promised a prize to the viewer who could correctly guess the exact date that the show would be canceled. One day the "David Letterman Show" celebrated Floyd Stiles Day. Who was Floyd Stiles? A retired janitor from Iowa. Another time, Letterman brought a television set onto his desk and faced it toward the camera so that he could show his viewers the programs on the other stations that they were missing. One morning, he asked someone in the studio audience to take his place as host while he left the stage for a while. Sometimes the wacky experimentation got out of control, as when a flock of sheep were brought onto the stage and started to go all over the place. But for Letterman, even the mistakes could be funny. "Ladies and gentlemen, what you are witnessing here is a good idea gone awry," Letterman announced. "Yes, a fun-filled surprise turning into an incredible screwup."

Producer Barry Sand described these weeks of working on the "David Letterman Show": "We were getting more and more absurd, and better and better—and going down in flames." But finally the inevitable happened, and on September 29, word came that the network was canceling the show. Though he had known it was coming, Letterman was dejected nonetheless. His dream was disappearing, despite the fact that, as he put it, "this is the hardest I've worked on anything in my life for any length of time. At least I now know in my heart that I did the best I could and tried the hardest." Knowing this, however, was little consolation, and Letterman later compared this period to "falling down an endless shaft into the miasma."

One irony of the cancellation was that it came when the show's ratings had actually started to go up. But the damage had been done—enough affiliates had dropped the show, and the network decided not to let it have its 26 weeks to evolve. A second irony of the cancellation was that after the show went off the air, it won two Emmy awards, which honor outstanding television programs—one to Letterman for best daytime talk show and one to Markoe for best achievement in writing.

But these accolades did nothing to ease the disappointment for Letterman, whose natural disposition was pessimistic and self-critical. As Markoe, who lived and worked with him, expressed, "He was pretty sure he would never work again. He's a pessimist, and this gave him a chance to be really pessimistic." Letterman's own thoughts backed this up: "I just figured my one shot on TV had come and gone and that's it and I would be destined to doing guest shots on 'The Love Boat' for the rest of my life."

Back in California, Letterman's life slowed down, but it did not stop, and it certainly did not become reduced to "Love Boat" cameos. He and Markoe settled back into

In May 1981, Letterman proudly holds the Emmy he was awarded for being top variety-show host despite the cancellation of his daytime show by NBC. The network axed the show because it finished in last place out of all the programs in its time slot (10:00 A.M. to 11:30 A.M.) and it was panned by most critics.

Letterman's Malibu house and began working on other assignments, including writing for several television projects. Letterman also made appearances on the "Tonight Show" and at comedy clubs, though he still did not enjoy performing live. At least Letterman did not have to worry about money. NBC renewed his contract, which paid him whether he worked or not. Even though the "David Letterman Show" had failed, the executives still believed they could use Letterman somehow. "Merrill and I just got used to the sudden inactivity and frustration," Letterman said, looking back at this time. "And even though I thought I would probably never get another shot on TV, I eventually started saying to myself, 'So what?' and went on with my life."

But Letterman was wrong—he was going to get another shot on television, and sooner than he thought. Many industry analysts believed that the low ratings of the "David Letterman Show" were due not to the content of the show but to the time slot in which the show aired. As producer Barry Sand put it, "Ten A.M. is the Bermuda triangle of time slots." (The Bermuda triangle is a region off the Florida Keys in the Atlantic Ocean known for the mysterious disappearances of ships and airplanes.)

From the beginning, many analysts both inside and outside the show had suspected that the time slot was inappropriate for several reasons. Comedy, especially innovative comedy, has traditionally not played well at that hour of the day. According to Letterman's bosses at NBC, housewives would not appreciate his brand of humor unless he made some adjustments, though many have argued this point and disagreed with the sexism implicit in this generalization. Markoe, for instance, said that the executives were "always telling me what women want to watch. They can't tell me. I have all the respect in the world for women." But even she conceded, "The morning show was just a delusion in the sense that we felt you could just do whatever comedy you wanted, any time of day or night."

When the show was canceled, an article in the *New York Times* seemed to sum up the prevailing feeling: "Letterman aficionados should be able to argue a case study in faulty scheduling. It is hard to imagine that there is not an audience, probably not housewives and perhaps late-night, for a talk show host whom critics have called one of the cleverest, quickest and least predictable comedians around."

Despite the opinions of the network executives, and despite Letterman's own feelings that "in truth, I'm not sure that this show is something you want to watch at ten in the morning," Letterman and Markoe had been committed to their style and format. Even as the ship was sinking, they stayed the course and made few compromises to their vision. In the end, it was the time slot that was changed, not the "David Letterman Show." A year and a half after the program went off the air, NBC gave Letterman a new show, to be broadcast at 12:30 A.M. It looked like Letterman had finally found his niche.

7 "Late Night with David Letterman"

LETTERMAN'S SECOND ATTEMPT at network television, "Late Night with David Letterman," started off much more positively than did his first. It received mixed reviews and decent ratings, both of which improved with time. This stronger showing was due in part to the new time slot, 12:30 A.M., just after the "Tonight Show." Not only did the new airtime attract an audience more in tune with Letterman's style of humor, but it also gave the show the benefit of the spillover audience from Johnny Carson's popular show. Arranging television schedules is much like setting the batting order on a baseball team, and a program's success is determined in part by the shows that come before and after it. The "Tonight Show," which had a large, established viewership, gave the Letterman show a starting audience. In addition, there was a small but loyal audience from Letterman's daytime show that followed him to the new time slot.

From the start, both the critical response and the ratings, 2.7 with a 14 percent share of the viewing households, were encouraging. To the network and its advertisers, these ratings were even better than they appeared, because

On January 19, 1982, Letterman announces that he will host a new show, "Late Night with David Letterman," which will follow the "Tonight Show" on NBC. The program was given the 12:30 A.M. time slot in hopes of attracting an audience that appreciated Letterman's kind of humor.

almost half of Letterman's audience was made up of 18- to 34-year-old viewers with largely disposable incomes. As advertisers know, these are the viewers inclined to spend the most on advertised products. Even with Letterman's natural tendency toward pessimism, he conceded that "this show will be harder to screw up than the last one. But by God," he added, "I'm gonna work around the clock to try."

The new time slot was only one reason for the improved response. The morning show had provided Letterman with valuable experience and allowed him to make mistakes and learn from them. When he organized the new show, Letterman surrounded himself with a professional team made up of trusted colleagues and practiced broadcasters who understood the kind of show he wanted to do and knew how to put it together. "We knew what we wanted to do and whom we wanted to do it with," Letterman said. "We brought Barry Sand back as producer—he'd been producing SCTV [Second City Television, a comedy show] in the meantime—and Markoe as head writer, and Hal Gurnee, a wonderful and extremely creative guy who, incidentally, used to be Jack Paar's director, to direct. We hired a small staff of bright, funny, sensitive people who never want to go to the Polo Lounge for Perrier."

When "Late Night with David Letterman" debuted on February 1, 1982, David Letterman joined an NBC tradition of late-night programming. Johnny Carson had long reigned as King of the Night; but there were other "Tonight Show" hosts who had helped define the genre. NBC was the network that had first developed the talk show in the 1950s. But even after the other networks aired similar productions, NBC remained dominant in late-night programming.

Although there is now a plethora of talk shows on the air, they were not always so plentiful. In fact, in the early days of television, they did not exist at all. Invented in the 1920s, television remained a novelty for the next 20 years while radio continued to fill the public's news and entertainment needs. Radio programming ran the gamut from music and variety shows to dramas and comedies featuring many of the most talented actors and performers of the time. At the 1939 New York World's Fair, RCA, one of the largest radio broadcasting companies in the country, demonstrated television sets and announced that they were ready to be purchased. The sets were expensive, however, and programming was sparse, as television networks were just forming. Two radio networks—the National Broadcasting Company (NBC), which was owned by RCA, and the Columbia Broadcasting System (CBS)—began operating television stations as well. By the 1950s, there were two more networks, the American Broadcasting Company (ABC), and the Du Mont Television Network (which eventually dissolved). At this point, television became a viable commercial enterprise and a threat to the popularity of radio. The excitement of invention and exploration captured the spirits of both those making and those watching the new medium, and the decade of the 1950s has become known as the Golden Age of Television.

At first, television programming borrowed directly from radio, and viewers could see the same types of programs on television that they could listen to on the radio. In some cases, they could see the same performers. Aside from news and information programs, the television studios produced variety shows, which featured comedy skits, music, and dance performances. Many of these shows were emceed by such personalities as Arthur Godfrey ("Talent Scouts") and Ted Mack ("Original Amateur Hour"), who had formerly hosted radio shows. Milton Berle, the comedian who hosted the "Texaco Star Theater," was the first major television star. His variety

Comedian Milton Berle, known as Uncle Miltie and Mr. Television, makes an appearance as a mountain climber on his show the "Texaco Star Theater." Berle liked to wear funny costumes on his variety show, which became a smash hit when it was first televised in 1948.

show premiered in 1948 and was so successful that Berle has since been known as Mr. Television. Other early television successes included Sid Caesar, who hosted "Your Show of Shows," and Ed Sullivan, whose variety program was on the air for 23 years.

Other types of early programming included music shows, which broadcast operas and symphonies; action stories, such as the "Lone Ranger," which had been on radio; dramas, which were essentially plays filmed for television; family situation comedies, now known as sitcoms; and children's shows, such as the "Howdy Doody Show," which premiered in 1947. During the 1950s, the range of programming expanded to include quiz shows—both the serious intellectual ones like "Down You Go" and the comedy-celebrity type such as "What's My Line?," in which celebrity panelists had to guess the guests' occupations, and "You Bet Your Life," hosted by movie comedian Groucho Marx. Soon there were spectaculars, which were music and comedy specials with big-name stars from theater and movies; made-for-television movies; episodic dramatic series, such as police and cowboy shows, in which the same characters would return each week; cultural and educational shows; sports, political, and journalistic programs like Edward R. Murrow's "Person to Person"; and the filmed situation comedies like "I Love Lucy," "Ozzie and Harriet," and the "Honeymooners," which have become classics of television's Golden Age.

In the 1950s, a new type of program, the talk show, was introduced. It had a simple format: celebrity guests would visit a host and chat informally and unrehearsed, sometimes offering a brief performance. Compared to other types of shows, the talk show was inexpensive to produce: it required only a simple set with a place for the host and guests to sit, and it sometimes featured a band. The chief executive at NBC during this time, Sylvester "Pat" Weaver, thought this magazine-style program would work well during the two time slots that attracted the fewest viewers: early morning and late night. The first morning talk show, NBC's "Today," debuted in 1952 and was initially hosted by David Garroway and later by Hugh Downs. Its informative, conversational tone set the parameters for magazine-format programs.

NBC proved to be the innovator in the nighttime talk show as well. In 1950, NBC's "Broadway Open House," hosted by Morey Amsterdam and then Jerry Lester, went on the air. Broadcast live, it was a variety show with a band and comedy skits, but it also featured informal chats with performers who, theoretically, were stopping by the studio after the close of their Broadway plays. Airing at 11:00 P.M., when not much else was on television, the show was popular until it went off the air about a year later. Though short lived, "Broadway Open House" helped pave the way for Steve Allen, a comedian and musician with radio broadcasting experience, to host a talk show on the New York NBC affiliate. Weaver and other NBC executives thought this type of show would do well all over the country and in 1954 the format went national with the "Tonight!" show, hosted by Steve Allen.

Allen opened the debut of "Tonight!" by announcing, "We especially selected this theater because it sleeps, I think, about eight hundred people. . . . This is kind of a mild little show. It's not a spectacular—monotony is more like it." Allen, whose versatile talents include composing music, writing books, and performing comedy, drama, and music, developed many of the basics that still define the late-night talk genre: the couch and desk arrangement; the opening comedy monologue; intelligent, witty conversation with a variety of guests, including actors, artists, and intellectuals; and performances by up-and-coming comedians, such as Lenny Bruce and Shelly Berman. He excelled at the ad-libbed comment and often went into the audience to interact with the crowd. One of his most famous shticks was "Stump the Band," in which he asked audience members to name obscure songs that the house band might not know how to play. Though Allen was known for his intelligence and quick wit, he also enjoyed physical comedy and often performed zany stunts. Once, he put on a specially made suit covered with tea bags and had himself lowered into a giant cup of hot water. In his "man-in-the-street" bits, Allen went on location in the streets of New York with a camera crew. Like Letterman years later, Allen prized the unexpected. "I think the heart of all humor is something gone wrong," he once said. On one occasion, two women in his studio audience were rudely talking throughout the taping of the show. Allen's reaction? "I slanted all my talk that night to these two old ladies. I could have had a page throw them out, but instead I made them part of the show."

One of Allen's frequent substitute hosts was Ernie Kovacs, an eccentric television comedian who also hosted radio and television shows of his own. Kovacs had a spirit of experimentation that was (and still is) unequaled in the field of television. While many of the pioneers in television borrowed forms and techniques from other mediums (radio, film, and theater), Kovacs's innovative comedy was made expressly for, and by, television. He worked with the technical aspects of television to create startling images and clever visual jokes. Once he designed the set to be tilted at a 20-degree angle and instructed the camera crew to tilt the cameras the same 20 degrees. On the screen, everything looked perfectly normal until Kovacs poured himself a cup of coffee and it came out sideways, seemingly defying gravity. Another time he designed a set that was built upside down, and then had the camera crew film him from an upside-down camera, thus creating the illusion that he was walking on the ceiling. He enjoyed revealing the gimmickry that most broadcasters try to hide. One time he had his guests stop talking in midsentence and freeze their body positions when a commercial interrupted them. When the commercial ended, and Kovacs and his guests came back on the screen, they unfroze and resumed the conversation right where they had left off. Like Steve Allen, Ernie Kovacs incorporated music into his shows, often in surprising ways, and the two of them together were the most innovative pioneers of television.

When Allen left the "Tonight!" show in 1957 to work full-time on another program, NBC filled the time slot briefly with a hodgepodge of programming and then returned to the "Tonight!" format with a new host, Jack Paar. Under Paar, the program was first called "Tonight" and then the "Jack Paar Tonight Show," but it maintained the basic formula started by Allen: an opening monologue, brief comedy sketches, and conversations with celebrities. Hal Gurnee, who served as director on both Paar's show and, years later, Letterman's show, once discussed the evolution of the "Tonight Show." With "Broadway Open House," he said, "The form was there; and each time a new show came along, it borrowed from the past. Jack Paar took the Steve Allen format and kind of formalized it. Paar made more of a conversation show than a kind of madcap, sketchy getting-people-on-the-telephone-late-at-night."

Paar, who was witty and personal, added an intimate tone to the program and hosted successfully for five years. Like Allen, his guests included great talkers and thinkers, but Paar focused more on popular celebrities and more on talking. As with the hosts before and after him, Paar downplayed his own show and once said, "The show is nothing. Just me and people talking. We don't act, we just defend ourselves." He was notorious for his unpredictability and on-air feuds with various other industry figures. Once, he announced on the air that he intended to quit the show because NBC refused to shorten its grueling one-hour-and-forty-five-minute running time. *Newsweek* summed up Paar's show as "Russian roulette

Jack Paar (left) became the host of the "Tonight Show" in 1957 after Steve Allen left to work full-time on another program. Paar is seen here getting tangled up in a fish net while program announcer Hugh Downs looks on. Paar made the program more of a conversation show than a zany program filled with comedy sketches.

with commercials." But the feuds only added to his popularity and helped give the show strong ratings during his tenure.

His popularity was so great that in 1962, when Paar left the "Tonight Show," no one could imagine a replacement. But Johnny Carson, who was then host of the ABC quiz show "Who Do You Trust?," stepped in and ended up staying 30 years. Carson was a comedian from the Midwest who had started out doing magic shows as a child, calling himself the "Great Carsoni." On the "Tonight Show," he maintained the familiar format and standards that had been set by the previous hosts. Though not an innovator, Carson was a witty comic and a charming conversationalist. He appeared in skits, played off straight man Ed McMahon, and delivered a clever, polished monologue every night, often commenting on topical and political events of the day's news.

By the late 1960s, Carson was as popular as his predecessors had been, and he had made some subtle but significant changes to the program. A staff of writers and a small group of actors joined the crew to assist Carson with his jokes and skits. The focus of the program remained on comedy, but Carson featured other performers as well, including singers, magicians, and animal trainers. There was also an increased emphasis on glamorous, show-business celebrities, which became even more prominent when Carson moved the show from New York to Los Angeles in 1972. The guests and entertainers, both newcomers and established stars, were all guided by the polite, confident manner of their host. Until 1992, when Carson retired, his "Tonight Show Starring Johnny Carson" was the preeminent showcase for comedians and other performers, and Carson was the most familiar television personality in the country.

"Late Night with David Letterman" reflected the rich history of NBC's late-night programming and borrowed elements from Allen, Kovacs, Paar, and Carson. Though Letterman was not taking on the "Tonight Show," he was nonetheless joining this illustrious line of comedians who had developed the concept of the nighttime comedy talk show. To this tradition, Letterman brought his own personality, style, and innovations.

Like Steve Allen, Letterman thrived on the unexpected, and his "Late Night with David Letterman" had the impromptu feel of a live show. Though it was videotaped in the early evening (at an NBC studio in New York's Rockefeller Center) and then replayed for broadcast, Letterman described the program as "a live show on videotape. You've got to keep the tape rolling no matter what; otherwise you lose that element of jeopardy."

From his opening remarks on the debut broadcast, it was clear that Letterman shared Allen's self-deprecating wit. "The fact that we're on at 12:30 at night by definition ought to create an air of excitement," Letterman announced. "Of course, that's an illusion—it's only television. We're not changing history—though we've got that scheduled for the second night."

He had other things in common with Allen as well. For instance, the remote videos, devised by Markoe and Letterman for the daytime show, were reminiscent of Allen's "man-on-the-street" episodes. But on "Late Night," these remotes took on an even wackier slant. Letterman used his wide-eyed midwestern attitude to expose the humor in the streets and establishments of New York City. A favorite topic was taxicabs and their drivers. But he also visited a Chinese restaurant because it had a signed picture of actor Alan Alda posted on the wall. In a mock-serious tone, Letterman questioned the staff on Alda's favorite dishes and how well he handled chopsticks. Another time Letterman "undercovered" what he called "the shame of the city," and took viewers on a tour of misspelled signs. In another remote, he

Ernie Kovacs, a pioneer in comedy for television, appears here as one of his many characters in the 1950s. Kovacs loved to work with the technical aspects of the medium, tilting cameras to create startling images and clever visual jokes.

visited a series of places named "Jimmy's"—pizza parlors, laundromats, stores, coffee shops—trying to track down "this guy called 'Jimmy.'"

Letterman was no actor, and, unlike Allen and Carson, he refused to dress up in costumes and play parts in comedy sketches. He did, however, enjoy stunts. Some of the crazier ones, reminiscent of Allen, involved donning suits made of sponges or Alka Seltzer tablets and immersing himself in vats of water, or wearing a suit made of Velcro and hurling himself at a wall made of the opposite side of the Velcro.

In other stunts, Letterman demonstrated an affinity with Ernie Kovacs, in both his tendency toward the bizarre and his interest in the technical aspects of televi-

95

sion. Since his college days, Letterman had liked to reveal the seams that most broadcasters take pains to keep hidden. On the "Late Show," he took advantage of the mobility of modern video equipment and often brought his camera crew on impromptu backstage tours. He had cameras mounted on the ceiling, as well as on monkeys, cows, and guests. On one show, the camera rotated 360 degrees, in 90-degree intervals, so that Letterman and his guests appeared sideways and, midway through the program, upside down.

What Letterman admired about Allen and Kovacs was their "casual kind of liveliness, an un-slick, see-the-camera-cable/see-the-mistakes kind of things. See, what we try to do is pure Television. . . . We go into the studio, use the cameras, invite the people in—we do a television show. Whereas what most other people do is produce things to be shown on television, but they're not Television—they're dramas, comedies, musicals, whatever. They're at the slick end of things and we're at the bargain basement end."

Like Allen and Kovacs, Letterman exhibited an excitement toward the possibilities of the television medium. But his style was distinguished by a childlike glee that showed itself in his on-air elevator races and in antics like dropping watermelons, typewriters, or water balloons out the window or off the roof of the RCA building, which houses the NBC studios. "It's every 14-year-old's dream of what he'd do if he had

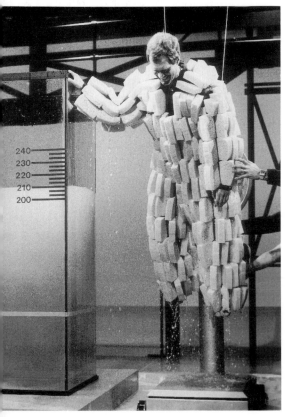

In 1985, on "Late Night with David Letterman," the host, wearing a suit of sponges, is taken out of a tank of water and placed on a scale to determine how much he weighs. Letterman incorporated many of the antics of his predecessors on late-night television into his show, including the crazy stunts of Allen and the celebrity interviews of Carson.

$100,000 and a big press to crush things," said "Late Night" director Hal Gurnee, referring to Letterman's penchant for subjecting bowling balls and Smurf dolls to steamrollers or hydraulic presses. "And everyone is tempted to drop things off a five-story building without worrying about the consequences." Letterman sometimes stuck his face right into the camera and often followed his stunts with slow-motion replays. His guests included the Doormen of the Year and officers from the best-dressed state police department (Rhode Island). On the Custom-made Show, he let the studio audience take over and design the program.

Paul Shaffer (left), bandleader of Letterman's late-night show, and political consultant Lee Atwater rehearse a musical number for the program. Letterman often teases Shaffer during the show, much like Carson joked with Doc Severinson on the "Tonight Show."

Letterman introduces Mary Kasan and her pet poodle "Bengy" during a segment of "stupid pet tricks" on "Late Night with David Letterman" in 1982. The stupid pet tricks idea had originated on Letterman's daytime show, but he continued the segment and even expanded it on his late-night show to include stupid human tricks.

"Late Night with David Letterman" seemed to be a talk show that was also a parody of a talk show. "I'm not a talk-show host," Letterman said in 1987, "but I play one on TV." Though he was following the general format established in the 1950s, he brought an overriding sarcasm to the conventions of television and to the talk show in particular. As "Late Night" staff writer Randy Cohen once explained, "A lot of Dave's humor is based on the assumption that what we're doing is trivial. Television is always making a big fuss about a small thing, and nobody is better at that than Dave. "Late Night" is silly and unimportant. Yet Dave is a *big* star, and we cash our *big* paychecks every week." His banter with bandleader Paul Shaffer, for instance, was reminiscent of Carson's banter with bandleader Doc Severinson or sidekick Ed McMahon. But with Shaffer, who almost seemed like a parody of a lounge singer himself, the banter had an edge of irony. This irony was not lost on the critics. Once the show had carved its niche and proven successful, *Time* magazine said, "Like 'Saturday Night Live' in the '70s, 'Late Night with David Letterman' has defined the cutting edge of TV comedy in the '80s: hip, irreverent, self-parodying, both scornful of and fascinated by the clichés of show business."

Throughout the years, however, Letterman has denied that his show is a parody. "It was never our intention to satirize or parody a talk show," he said in 1989. "It's just that we have an hour of TV to do each night, and it's got to be a talk show, so what can we do inside that framework that would make us laugh? It's just goofy, silly, additional behavior. We never said 'What we want to do here is construct a mirror of the American talk show and hold that up to the viewer.' We never really set out to show people a parody of the talk show. I mean it *is* a talk show."

Another time he pointed out that his show "has exactly the structure of Merv [Griffin, another talk-show host] and Johnny [Carson] and all the others. I sit at a desk and guests come out." Though "Late Night" certainly fit into the talk-show category, it was more about comedy than it was about talking. Writer Cohen, who helped develop the 360-degree show, believed, "Television should enter-

Letterman reunited Sonny and Cher, the former singing duo and former husband and wife, during a "Late Night" interview. Several of Letterman's guests have caused controversy before the cameras, including Madonna (who used foul language) and actress Drew Barrymore (who took off her blouse).

tain, inform, and irritate." This seemed to reflect Letterman's philosophy as well. "We want viewers at home to look at each other and say, 'What the hell was that?'" he once said. "We want to pierce that flat TV screen."

In this effort, Letterman introduced a number of innovations to the nighttime talk show genre. The stupid pet tricks, which had debuted on the daytime show, continued on the late-night show and expanded to include stupid human tricks, which presented people with odd, sometimes disgusting, talents. "Late Night" also hosted visits from a cast of unusual people, including Larry "Bud" Melman, a cantankerous older man who

was so realistic many people did not realize he was a character played by actor Calvert DeForest.

In 1985, Letterman read off a list of the "Top Ten Things That Almost Rhyme with Peas," a gimmick that soon became a trademark of the Letterman show. Presented nightly, the Top Ten list was a "mixture of high-brow with nonsense," according to writer Steve O'Donnell, who came up with the idea. Topics for the lists have included the top ten numbers from one to ten, the top ten pickup lines for Vice-President Dan Quayle, and the top ten reasons to stop doing the Top Ten. Over the years the Top Ten list has become for Letterman what the monologue was for Carson on the "Tonight Show." It began appearing in newspapers and on the computer Internet for those who missed it the night before, and several collections of the Top Ten lists have been compiled into books.

Though Letterman had always admired Johnny Carson and shared his talents for ad-libbing, his own style was very different. Carson, who was smooth, suave, and entrenched in the celebrity-filled world of Hollywood, was at ease chatting with the big-name stars who came on as his guests. Jack Paar had also been adept at the celebrity interview and gave the impression that he was close friends with many of his guests. But Letterman did not share this cozy attitude toward the rich and famous. His manner was often awkward, especially in the early years, and sometimes antagonistic, and he had no tolerance for what he considered superficial or self-promoting conversation. "When I think about television and show business, it grinds my stomach," he said in 1988. "I want to say to people, 'Don't you understand this is just [nonsense], driven by egos, and that's all it is?' I mean nothing makes me madder than to be sitting there, watching somebody who's just the winner of the genetic crapshoot, and there they are, big stuff on the air, a *star*."

Unlike Carson, who was impeccably groomed and had a succession of beautiful wives and famous girl-friends, Letterman wore sneakers and jeans on and off the air and lived a blatantly unglamorous life. True to his roots, he aligned himself with the regular working person, and his jokes sprang from this point of view. He often referred to his hometown, his alma mater, and his mother. Even as his popularity grew, he avoided celebrity circles and worked hard to maintain his persona as an average guy. "Privately, I think that I'm not really some-body who has a network television show," he said. "Ce-lebrities are other people—Johnny Carson and Sylvester Stallone. I'm just a kid trying to make a living."

In fact, Letterman's anticelebrity attitude sometimes showed itself in what some critics have called a mean streak. At first, his interviewing style just seemed unusual, perhaps inexperienced. But he soon earned a reputation as a difficult conversationalist who could be insulting toward his guests, most of whom were accustomed to pandering interviewers. But Letterman has contended time and time again that his goal is to entertain, not to humiliate. "I'm not malicious," he once said. "I don't want to get a laugh at the expense of others. . . . Then again, if I see an opening, I go for it." In a 1989 *Time* magazine interview, he elaborated. In response to writer Richard Zoglin's assertion that "some viewers find you condescending, smug, even mean," Letterman said:

> I suppose I am all of those things, but we never invite somebody on to demonstrate condescension—or conden-sation. If somebody comes on and is a bonehead and is loafing through an interview, I resent that, and maybe I will then go after them. But if you come on and are polite and well groomed and behave yourself, then you've got nothing to worry about. I'm stunned at the number of people in show business who come on and don't seem to get that what we want from them is a performance, you

know, tell us three stories out of your life. Anybody who has been on this planet 20 years and doesn't have three stories, well, they should re-examine what they're doing.

It used to trouble me that people thought our sole purpose for being in business was to make fun of people. Unfortunately, there is no joke that does not make fun of somebody. I try to make it, as often as not, me or the show or somebody in our little group. So if we do say something that looks like we're making fun of somebody else, it's in the spirit of everything. But some people don't buy that. I know that some people can't stand me, and it troubles me because I think we're just trying to do the funniest show we know how.

Unlike many television personalities, Letterman seemed to be uninterested, or perhaps unable, to court favor with people in power. He had never had any tolerance for people he thought were "phony," and though he was sometimes criticized for a tactless demeanor, he had many fans who appreciated this directness. One of Letterman's most famous feuds was not with a celebrity; it was with his employers, the General Electric (GE) company, which bought NBC in 1986. Like Jack Paar's on-air feuds, this one did not hinder the show's ratings: there were many disgruntled workers who must have gotten a vicarious pleasure out of Letterman's fearless attacks on his employers. When Letterman took a camera crew and a basket of fruit to welcome his new bosses, he met up with a series of rude security personnel who barred him from entering the building or meeting any GE executives. Broadcast on "Late Night with David Letterman," this scene put the joke on GE and began a long-lasting series of on-air jabs at the company.

Letterman had other targets as well. Over the years, he has picked on such figures as Vice-President Dan Quayle, "Today" show cohost Bryant Gumbel, and newsmaker Joey Buttafuoco, often repeating their names over and over during a broadcast. For some critics, his humor was not just youthful but immature. According to an article in *Vanity Fair,* his mental attitude was "not just collegiate but undergraduate. Intellectually, he's never left the dorm—he's still playing hall hockey with a rolled-up pair of socks." For others, his attitude seemed to come from the fraternity house, and his staff of writers—all 20- and 30-year-old white men—was considered to be too homogeneous. One former "Late Night" writer concurred: "It was like working in a frat. All the writers were men but Merrill. It was very sexist. . . . In some ways Letterman is real square."

Nonetheless, for Letterman, who has been called "an angry guy for an angry age" and "a crabby guy for a crabby time," this crankiness may have been a crucial factor in his popularity. Though his behavior veered toward rudeness at times, he exhibited a directness that many found refreshing. Not many people who make a living on television would admit that it is permeated with "so much phony effervescence and so much phony joy," as Letterman did to television critic Tom Shales. But as Shales has suggested, Letterman's average, boy-next-door persona may have been key to making his anger more palatable. Of all the talk-show hosts, Shales believes that "Letterman is the mellowest and most neighborly yet. He's a cutup, he's a caution, but you'd welcome him at a barbecue or church supper. He'd be good playing baseball with nuns."

Letterman continued to align himself with the average American even after his income and popularity put him squarely into the rich-and-famous category. Just two years after its debut, "Late Night with David Letterman" had earned a steady viewership of about 4 million households per night, including many of the 20-year-old to 30-year-old men with the disposable incomes so attractive to advertisers. In 1984, daytime talk-show host Phil Donahue aired a celebration of Letterman's life, helping

to confirm his celebrity status. In 1986, Letterman commemorated the sixth anniversary of "Late Night" with a star-studded show at New York's Radio City Music Hall. That same year he served as cohost of the nationally televised Emmy Awards ceremony. By 1988, Letterman himself had been awarded eight Emmys and television critics were calling "Late Night" "the comedy show of the eighties, the one that defines television humor the way 'Saturday Night Live' did in the seventies and Sid Caesar's 'Your Show of Shows' did in the fifties."

"Late Night with David Letterman" was the focus of Letterman's life, and he spent most of his waking hours working on the show. He was a perfectionist, notoriously

Letterman waves to the audience astride a white horse he rode off the set of "Late Night" on the last show on NBC. Letterman aligned himself with the average American even after his income and popularity made him a rich celebrity—by 1992, his show earned $55 million per year for NBC.

self-critical and always striving to improve his program. Merrill Markoe once explained, "He's a lot more worried than he looks and a lot less easygoing than you think." Every evening after the show was taped and edited, Letterman would go into his office and watch it, looking for his mistakes. This self-review was an integral part of his working day. "I have my own little ritual," he once said. "But I should. If you've got men on base and you can't drive them in, how come you're getting major league money?" Though he also said that after a poor performance, "you come back the next day and try it again," Letterman was fully absorbed in his work and his self-criticism was often severe.

For Markoe, who lived and worked with Letterman, there was little relief from the "Late Night" show. She said at the time, "We go to dinner at night and we talk about the show. We wake up in the morning and we talk about the show. We promised ourselves that we were going to try to have a life this time and that after the show was over, it would be an off-limits subject, so that you would have a normalized situation. But it hasn't worked out that way." In later years, Letterman concurred, noting, "We were working on [the] show and then went home, and instead of having a life, we were still working on the show."

In 1982, Markoe tried to remedy the situation by removing herself from the position of head writer. Staff writer Steve O'Donnell took her place, and Markoe became an associate producer, in charge of the remote films and the pet segments. But this change did not improve things by much. In 1987, Markoe left the show altogether and moved back to Los Angeles, which she preferred to New York. For many years, she had given Letterman her creative energy and her best jokes, and she felt it was now time to pursue her own interests. Though Letterman and Markoe no longer worked together, they maintained their personal relationship for several years, even while living on opposite coasts. This arrangement did not last, however, and they eventually stopped seeing each other altogether. As Markoe later said, it was "a very bitter, sad, horrible breakup," and for many years they did not speak to one another. Letterman, who takes "full responsibility for the unhappiness and the unpleasant feelings that lingered," never stopped crediting Markoe for all her contributions to creating and developing the unique style of his television programs. "She is largely responsible for the success of the show, many of her ideas are mainstays, and she is one of the most important people in my life, ever." In 1994, Letterman said, "She's the funniest person I've ever met. And she's so smart it's scary. I mean she'd walk into a room and you could feel a hum coming out of her brain. She had some of the best pure ideas for TV that I've ever seen."

As "Late Night with David Letterman" continued to grow in popularity, Letterman persisted in clinging to his image as a regular guy. He bought a home in suburban New Canaan, Connecticut, and commuted to work; he kept regular hours, spending most of his time on his work and very little of it socializing. But by 1992, his show was earning $55 million dollars per year for NBC and it was being called "the hippest thing in television" by comedian Eddie Murphy and others. Twenty-five million people watched the 10th anniversary special, which was broadcast during prime time. David Letterman was no longer average.

Network Politics and a New "Late Show"

8

FOR ALMOST 10 YEARS, Letterman worked happily, if obsessively, on the "Late Night" program. But on May 23, 1991, when Johnny Carson announced his retirement from television, effective the following spring, it reignited the media's speculations on who would become the next host of the "Tonight Show." The rumors, which often named Letterman as a top contender, had been circulating for a decade. Letterman's usual response was to praise Carson and deny any interest in succeeding him. In 1986, he admitted, "In the back of my mind, if I weren't asked someday to do it, I'd feel kind of sad. Yet, doing it—that's my worst nightmare. That I'd be foolish enough to take Carson's position if offered to me, that I'd die a miserable death in that time slot, and meanwhile NBC had given my old show to someone who was quite happy to keep doing it."

Though he had mixed feelings for many years, by the time Carson announced his retirement, Letterman felt ready to take on the challenge of the "Tonight Show" and succeed Carson, Paar, and Allen, who had all served as role models for him. Letterman was proud to be a part of the long history

On January 14, 1993, Letterman pumps his fist during a press conference to announce his moving to CBS. After Carson's retirement, Letterman felt prepared to assume the Carson mantle on the "Tonight Show." NBC, however, decided to hire Jay Leno instead, thus causing what became known as the battle for late-night television.

of broadcasting that NBC represented, and hosting the "Tonight Show" seemed to him, and to many others in the television business, to be the logical next step.

The executives at NBC, however, soon announced that comedian Jay Leno would be the new host of the "Tonight Show." While Letterman had been busy hosting his "Late Night" show, Leno had become Carson's most frequent substitute. The network was pleased with Leno's performance and decided to make it permanent. Leno was also helped by his agent, Helen Kushnick, who had been quietly but forcefully negotiating with the NBC executives for several years. Furthermore, according to

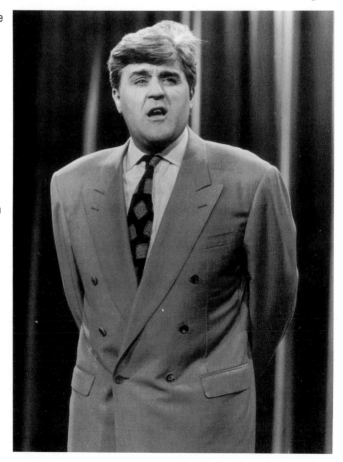

Jay Leno does his monologue as guest host of the "Tonight Show" in 1992. Letterman was insulted that he had not even been told by NBC executives that he had been passed over as Carson's replacement. Although Letterman had long admired Leno's comic talent, he truly believed that after 10 years of making money for the network he should have been asked to host the show.

Bill Carter, author of *The Late Shift: Letterman, Leno, and the Network Battle for the Night,* Leno was skilled in the kind of social and political maneuvering that Letterman disdained. While Leno had been making friends at NBC and its affiliate stations throughout the country, Letterman had antagonized many of his network bosses, both on and off the air.

Having two popular comedians, Leno and Letterman, in back-to-back shows would make a winning combination, and the NBC executives thought they had arranged a programming dream come true. But they did not take into account Letterman's feelings. At first, he expressed no ill will at the news that he had not been chosen to replace Carson. But eventually disappointment overtook him. He was insulted that he had been passed over and that the NBC chiefs had not bothered to tell him personally. He had, after all, given NBC more than 10 years of hard work and developed a popular, money-making program for the network. Letterman, now 44 years old, wanted to move out of the late-late-night slot and into the more accessible, mainstream time slot. "I'm too old to be on at 12:30," he said. "No one's watching. *I'm* too tired to watch—not tired of being on at 12:30, because I'm lucky to have had a job for this long in television. It's all I've ever really wanted to do. I just feel in order to extend my career, my public life, I've got to make this change." In a 1995 interview with CNN's talk-show host Larry King, Letterman explained, "At the time it seemed like it was 'The Tonight Show' or I was out of business. I couldn't stay at 12:30—I had been there."

After discussions with his colleagues and producers, Letterman decided to take action. What he most wanted was to host the "Tonight Show," but if NBC was not going to give him that job, he was not sure he wanted to continue working the late shift at the network. To explore his options, he enlisted the help of one of the most powerful negotiators in the entertainment business, agent Michael Ovitz of Creative Artists Agency. Ovitz let it be known that his client was considering not returning to NBC when his contract ran out in April 1993 and was therefore interested in other offers.

Thus began the most publicized network battle in recent history. Letterman, through his new agent, received offers from each of the other networks, plus a host of syndicate broadcasters. In the end, CBS, which was eager to have a late-night show to air against NBC's popular "Tonight Show," made the most attractive bid, and the war was on. Aside from a large sum of money, both in salary and in production budget, CBS promised Letterman ownership of his program through his production company, and, most significantly, the 11:30 P.M. time slot. As Carter explained in *The Late Shift*, Letterman's contract with NBC allowed the network to retain him as long as it met or exceeded the best offer he received elsewhere. In order to keep Letterman, the NBC executives not only had to match CBS's money offer but also had to give him the 11:30 time slot, which they had already promised to Jay Leno.

The plight of "Dave" and "Jay," as the two stars became known, soon emerged as the hottest topic in the news, and it made headlines in newspapers, magazines, and, of course, on television news broadcasts. Would Dave leave NBC for CBS? Would NBC replace Leno with Letterman? Would CBS make a pitch for Leno? These questions became a national obsession. The obsession went even beyond national borders. In Botswana, a tour guide approached NBC news anchor Tom Brokaw and asked, "Do you think Letterman is going to CBS?"

Many strange twists and bizarre episodes took place, including one during which Jay Leno hid in a closet in order to listen to a phone call between NBC executives discussing his fate. But finally the politics subsided and

the battle came to an end. Leno would remain the new host of the "Tonight Show." A worrier by nature, Letterman had agonized over whether he should leave NBC, but the CBS offer was too good to pass up. Soon Letterman's show would appear opposite the very program that had launched his career.

But the publicity did not end there. After the NBC–CBS battle was settled, there was a smaller battle between the cities of Los Angeles and New York, each trying to attract Letterman and his production. In New York, Mayor David Dinkins promised to do anything, including "back-flips off my eyebrows," to keep Letterman in his city. After Letterman elected to remain there, most of the publicity focused on whether Letterman would sink or swim at the new time slot and on CBS's efforts to refurbish the Ed Sullivan Theater, which the network had

On January 14, 1993, Letterman talks about his multimillion-dollar deal to host a late-night show for CBS. Seated at the right of Letterman is Laurence Tisch, president and CEO of the CBS network. Letterman's new show would run against NBC and Jay Leno's "Tonight Show" at 11:30 P.M.

During Letterman's debut on CBS, on August 30, 1993, actor and comedian Bill Murray spray paints Letterman's desk at the Ed Sullivan Theater in New York. Letterman had to change certain elements of the show's format because NBC executives regarded the stupid pet tricks, the Top Ten list, and the Larry "Bud" Melman character the "intellectual property" of NBC.

purchased for the broadcast of Letterman's new show. The next big question was: Who would win the ratings battle when David Letterman's show went up against Jay Leno's?

By the time the "Late Show with David Letterman" debuted on CBS on August 30, 1993, Letterman had become the focus of so much publicity that even he was sick of seeing his own image on television, billboards, and magazine covers. CBS had added to the publicity with what Letterman described as a "round-the-clock promo campaign. I mean, God bless them. But after a while it was choking."

Though CBS's "Late Show" had much in common with NBC's "Late Night," there were some significant differences. Some of these changes emanated from the

feeling, held by Letterman, his staff, and many in the television business, that the earlier time slot required a different approach. Since Letterman began vying for an 11:30 P.M. program, many critics suggested that his style of comedy and his on-air manner would not do well at the earlier time, with its older, more mainstream audience. But Letterman insisted that he was not only able to, but eager to, make the adjustment. "I think this is just a great opportunity for us to apply 11 years of experience to try to build the best version of this show we can," he said. On the "Late Show," Letterman introduced a new look for both himself—a fashionable suit instead of jeans and a sport coat—and for his program, which was enhanced by high-tech graphics and artwork.

But some of the changes to Letterman's show were mandated by a threat from NBC's legal department. Letterman's former bosses made it clear that because NBC owned "Late Night with David Letterman," it also owned many of the elements of that show. Even though Letterman, Markoe, and the writing staff had created stupid pet tricks, the Top Ten list, and the Larry "Bud" Melman character, NBC executives claimed these were the "intellectual property" of the network, and that Letterman could not use them on another network. Although the claim that something called "stupid pet tricks" could be termed "intellectual property" made NBC the laughingstock of the press, the executives were serious about their domain. As Letterman joked, "According to NBC lawyers, they own everything, including my peacock petting zoo [the peacock is the NBC mascot]."

On the debut of the CBS show, Letterman poked fun at his old network with an appearance by NBC anchor Tom Brokaw, who took a cue card from the set, claiming it was the "intellectual property" of NBC. Nonetheless, the "Late Show" did have to make some concessions to

On September 12, 1994, Letterman volleys with tennis professional Andre Agassi (who is off-camera) in the streets of New York during the taping of the "Late Show." Letterman continues to include remote "on the street" segments for the show.

avoid legal trouble. The house band could no longer be called the World's Most Dangerous Band, as it had been known on NBC, and the Larry "Bud" Melman character now had to use his real name of Calvert DeForest. In addition, the look of the Top Ten list was altered and enhanced by special graphics and effects, to make it distinct from the version Letterman had done on NBC.

Both the ratings and the critical response to the "Late Show with David Letterman" started off with a bang and remained strong. Going up at the same time as the "Tonight Show with Jay Leno," there was a built-in competition between the two programs, and their ratings and popularity were often compared. In the first few weeks, Letterman's show earned a 6.0 rating (compared with 4.0 for the "Tonight Show"), even though 30 percent of the CBS affiliates did not air the "Late Show" until after their local programming. In other words, Letterman was handicapped by both local programming interruptions as well as CBS's weaker prime-time lineup, but he still pulled in strong ratings that were consistently higher than Jay Leno's. In his first year with CBS, Letterman earned the network $140 million dollars from advertisers. By January 1995, the "Late Show" was maintaining an average rating of 5.6 (compared with 4.7 for the "Tonight Show"), and many critics were hailing Letterman as the new King of the Night.

But Letterman was not without his detractors. At this point, and throughout his career, there were those who thought his humor was sophomoric and his on-air behavior rude. But with the new show, Letterman began to be criticized by the people who had always appreciated those qualities in him. Some of his long-term fans felt that the "new" Letterman had lost some of his renegade qualities and was no longer edgy or caustic enough. CBS president Howard Stringer claimed that he did not want to turn his newest star into "a defanged Letterman or a blander Letterman," but even Letterman had started thinking, "Maybe people don't want you dropping water balloons off the building at 11:30," and vowed to make the new show "as appealing to as many people as possible."

Letterman's new popularity created an interesting dilemma: What happens when a person who has built a career out of being a "regular guy" becomes a full-fledged celebrity? Letterman certainly had all the signs of wealth and fame. Though he refused to disclose the exact amount of his new salary, estimates put it at $14 million per year, and he freely admitted that "I am overpaid." He purchased an 88-acre estate in Westchester County, New York, and also owned a loft in Manhattan and a collection of classic cars.

Though he still protected his privacy and did not talk much about his personal relationships, he granted interviews with a variety of magazines, and his picture continued to appear regularly at newsstands. In 1992, he let broadcast journalist Barbara Walters interview him on television. *Rolling Stone* magazine crowned him "Man of the Year" for 1994. And in 1995, this anticelebrity acted as host of the ultimate celebrity affair, the Academy Awards.

But even as David Letterman was becoming more of a celebrity, he hung onto his renegade attitude. At the Academy Awards, for instance, Letterman, surrounded by hundreds of movie stars and paparazzi, presented a stupid pet trick (a "self-winding dog" who ran in circles when the audience applauded); a remote tape featuring cab drivers talking about movies; and a Top Ten list of "signs that the movie you're watching will not win an Academy award." Apparently, though he was hosting a different show, he had no intentions of changing his style or his content. While some people found his Oscar-night attitude refreshing, many media critics believed it was out of place.

On his own show, Letterman also continued to align himself with the average American and emphasize his midwestern, middle-class persona. He endeared himself to many viewers when he hired his mother as the official "Late Show" correspondent to the 1994 Olympics in Lillehammer, Norway. Long-term fans had already been introduced to Letterman's mother on the Parents Night episode of NBC's "Late Night," and her nightly appearance during the Olympics was one more sign that the new Letterman was in many ways just the old Letterman in nicer clothing. (Her appearance also helped boost the show's ratings to an all-time high of 8.9.)

As for his not-very-average salary, Letterman either downplayed it or made fun of it. "I've never been motivated by money in my entire life," Letterman told Larry King in 1995. "I came from a background where we didn't have much money, but we didn't *want* much. So it was never really a factor. I'm lucky that I make a comfortable living and I can do nice things for my family, I can do nice things for my friends, and I can do nice things for people who don't have that kind of money, and that's the extent of it. It's not like, 'Ya-hoo, I've got money now, it's gonna be babes, babes, baabes.'"

According to Peter Lassally, who worked as a producer on both the "Tonight Show Starring Johnny Carson" and the "Late Show," Letterman's average-guy persona was for real: "Letterman approaches the business—and I think that's why he's so successful—like a civil service job. He works. He's here early in the morning, he has lunch

at his desk out of a tinfoil pan, he leaves late at night."
Others have concurred. Actress Teri Garr, a frequent
guest on Letterman's show, said, "Dave's a regular,
middle-class, ordinary guy who doesn't like it when you
spill Coca-Cola on his new carpet. Now he's been thrown
into this incredible thing, and he doesn't want to become
Elvis."

As Letterman told King, "I've always thought of myself as somebody who was in broadcasting, not necessarily
show business. And I'm more comfortable with that. And
if the two overlap, and I guess they do, then that's fine."

While critics were proclaiming that he "has rewritten
the rule book for the TV talk show, giving the form a hip,
self-satirizing edge, perfectly pitched to the baby boom
generation," Letterman was scoffing. "We were never

On March 27, 1995, Letterman introduces Sadie the dog as she performs a stupid pet trick during the annual Academy Awards ceremony in Los Angeles, while actor Tom Hanks, nominated for Best Actor in the film *Forrest Gump*, watches the trick. Letterman received mixed reviews from critics about how he hosted the event; he treated the show as though it were his late-night show and did not change his style or format.

hip," he proclaimed. "We're just people who come to work every day and do comedy, the same way people come to work at the library."

Though his work ethic was proletarian, Letterman realized that his job was anything but regular. Interviewed at his new Ed Sullivan Theater office, he said, "Every day I come in here I think I'm the luckiest man alive. It's a brand-new office. To me it's huge. I look down on Broadway. You know, I used to have a paper route. I don't know how this happened." Not everyone gets to see their childhood dream come true, and Letterman, who has said, "This is all I ever really wanted to do—have my own TV show," knew how fortunate he was. In his 1995 interview with King, he said, "I've had great fortune to work all my adult life in broadcasting, which is what I decided I wanted to do one day in high school, and who among us can say that? That they've been able to do exactly what they wanted to do all their lives?"

Letterman also knew "how unhappy and sad I would be if I didn't have a show to do every night." Nothing has ever mattered to him as much as his work, and throughout his career he has maintained that "I'm just the happiest, the best I ever feel, from five-thirty to six-thirty [when he tapes his program]." In 1994 he asserted, "It's certainly the most exciting hour of the day, and it's the only hour of the day I really care about. And if it goes well, you can't wait to do it again because it dumps so much adrenaline into your system. If it's going well, it just lifts you. If it's not going well, it sinks you. It's exhilarating. It's my favorite part of the day."

In the end, the paradox of being both a regular guy and a big-time celebrity does not seem to have posed much of a dilemma for Letterman. His serious and diligent approach to his job, like that of a librarian or civil servant, may be part of the explanation. But another part is his very unserious attitude toward his line of work. Though Letterman has worked in television for many years and enjoyed watching it for many more, he has always maintained a lighthearted perspective toward the medium. The foundation of his humor and his broadcasting style is summed up in the phrase "It's only television," which he has repeated many times over the years. Raised by parents who disdained television and discouraged their children from wasting time with it, Letterman has carried that view with him. "I think television stinks," he once said, "and I think it's supposed to stink. I don't think we want it to be good. There are exceptions, of course, but by and large, I don't think we want it to be so good that people spend any more time watching it. I think it's just about the way it ought to be."

Unlike other television personalities, Letterman has always maintained that television is inherently unimportant and not worth all the fuss that surrounds it. He has never lost sight of the fundamental commercialism of the medium. It is not surprising that someone with such an understanding of the pitfalls of the medium would have reservations about achieving success in it. "I'm not so sure that to succeed in that [American television] is such a pat on the back," he once said. Though he appreciates and enjoys his job and works hard to do the best he can, he nonetheless believes, "There's no great satisfaction in succeeding in television. What good is it? . . . It's not much of an accomplishment, really. That's why we try to take it in stride." In other words, it's only television.

Further Reading ★ ★ ★ ★ ★ ★ ★ ★ ★ ★ ★ ★ ★ ★ ★

Adler, Bill. *The Letterman Wit.* New York: Carroll & Graf, 1994.

Carter, Bill. *The Late Shift: Leno, Letterman, and the Network Battle for the Night.* New York: Hyperion, 1994.

Castleman, Harry, and Walter J. Podrazik. *Watching TV: Four Decades of American Television.* New York: McGraw-Hill, 1982.

Cox, Stephen. *Here's Johnny.* New York: Harmony Books, 1992.

Henderson, Amy. *On the Air: Pioneers of American Broadcasting.* Washington, DC: Smithsonian Institution Press, 1988.

Latham, Caroline. *The David Letterman Story.* New York: Franklin Watts, 1987.

Lennon, Rosemarie. *David Letterman: On Stage and Off.* New York: Windsor, 1994.

Parish, James Robert. *Let's Talk: America's Favorite Talk Show Hosts.* Las Vegas, NV: Pioneer Books, 1993.

Pooley, Eric. "Dave's Kids: The Twisted Minds Behind the Letterman Show." *New York,* January 19, 1987, 37–39.

Schruers, Fred. "David Letterman: Man of the Year." *Rolling Stone,* December 29, 1994, 34.

Settel, Irving, and William Lass. *A Pictorial History of Television.* New York: Grosset & Dunlap, 1969.

Verna, Tony. *Live TV: An Inside Look at Producing and Directing.* Stoneham, MA: Focal Press, 1987.

Winship, Michael. *Television.* New York: Random House, 1988.

Zehme, Bill. "David Letterman: The Rolling Stone Interview." *Rolling Stone,* February 18, 1993, 32.

Zoglin, Richard. "Dave Makes the Deal." *Time,* January 25, 1993, 62.

———. "He's No Johnny Carson." *Time,* February 6, 1989, 66–68.

Chronology ★ ★ ★ ★ ★ ★ ★ ★ ★ ★ ★ ★ ★ ★ ★ ★ ★ ★ ★

April 12, 1947 David Michael Letterman is born in Indianapolis, Indiana

1961 Enters Broad Ripple High School; gets a job at the Atlas Supermarket

1965 Moves to Muncie, Indiana, to attend Ball State University, where he majors in radio and television broadcasting; joins the Sigma Chi fraternity

1966–68 Forms the Dirty Laundry Company, a comedy troupe, with three friends; gets a job as a disc jockey at WBST, a campus radio station, and is subsequently fired; hired by WAGO, another campus station

1969 Marries fellow Ball State student Michelle Cook; graduates from Ball State and moves back to Indianapolis to work as an announcer and a weekend weatherman at television station WLWI–Channel 13

1974 Quits his job at station WLWI to host call-in talk show on Indianapolis radio station WNTS; his father dies

1975 Letterman moves, with his wife, Michelle, to Los Angeles, California, to pursue a network television career; he performs stand-up comedy at the Comedy Store, a Los Angeles nightclub

1977 Letterman and Michelle divorce

1978 Letterman is hired as a comedy writer and cast member on a short-lived network program that stars actress Mary Tyler Moore; he meets comedy writer Merrill Markoe, and develops a personal and professional relationship with her; performs comedy on the "Tonight Show Starring Johnny Carson," on November 26

1979 Signs contract with the NBC television network

1980 The "David Letterman Show" debuts on NBC during the morning time slot but is canceled after four months

1981 The "David Letterman Show," although no longer on the air, receives two Emmy awards for the previous season

1982 "Late Night with David Letterman" debuts on NBC in the late-night time slot that follows the "Tonight Show"

1984 "Late Night with David Letterman" viewership reaches 4 million

1987 Merrill Markoe leaves the show and moves back to Los Angeles; Letterman and Markoe end their personal relationship

1988 Letterman celebrates sixth anniversary of "Late Night with David Letterman" by broadcasting from New York City's Radio City Music Hall

1991 Disappointed with NBC for not giving him the "Tonight Show" position upon host Johnny Carson's retirement, Letterman considers changing networks

1993 "Late Show with David Letterman" debuts on CBS opposite NBC's "Tonight Show"

1995 Serves as host for the Academy Awards ceremony

Index ★

Frances Lefkowitz is a filmmaker and writer. Author of the Chelsea House biography *Marilyn Monroe,* she has also published short stories in *Fiction, Northeast Journal, Imagine,* and *The Pikestaff Forum.* In 1991, the Rhode Island State Council on the Arts awarded her the Fellowship in Literature and a grant in filmmaking. Born and raised in San Francisco, California, she earned a B.A. in anthropology from Brown University in Providence, Rhode Island, and currently lives in Kennebunkport, Maine.

Leeza Gibbons is a reporter for and cohost of the nationally syndicated television program "Entertainment Tonight" and NBC's daily talk show "Leeza." A graduate of the University of South Carolina's School of Journalism, Gibbons joined the on-air staff of "Entertainment Tonight" in 1984 after cohosting WCBS-TV's "Two on the Town" in New York City. Prior to that, she cohosted "PM Magazine" on WFAA-TV in Dallas, Texas, and on KFDM-TV in Beaumont, Texas. Gibbons also hosts the annual "Miss Universe," "Miss U.S.A.," and "Miss Teen U.S.A." pageants, as well as the annual Hollywood Christmas Parade. She is active in a number of charities and has served as the national chairperson for the Spinal Muscular Atrophy Division of the Muscular Dystrophy Association; each September, Gibbons cohosts the National MDA Telethon with Jerry Lewis.